PROFIT POWER: MASTERING THE ART OF MAKING MONEY

SHARON LARSON

TABLE OF CONTENT

ACKNOWLEDGEMENT
About the Author
COPYRIGHT
Book Description:
Introduction: Unlocking the Profit Power
Chapter 1: The Mindset of Wealth
Chapter 2: The Fundamentals of Profit
Chapter 3: The Power of Financial Literacy
Chapter 4: Building a Profitable Business - Introduction
Chapter 5: Effective Marketing and Sales Strategies
Chapter 6: Managing Finances for Profitability
Chapter 7: Investing for Long-Term Profit
Chapter 8: Leveraging Technology for Profit
Chapter 9: Navigating Economic Cycles and Trends
Chapter 10: Building Wealth and Leaving a Legacy
Conclusion: Embracing the Profit Power Mindset

ACKNOWLEDGEMENT

Writing a book of this nature requires the support and contributions of many individuals who have played a significant role in its creation. We would like to express our heartfelt gratitude to the following people:

First and foremost, we would like to thank our families for their unwavering support throughout this journey. Your love, encouragement, and understanding have been instrumental in bringing this book to life.

To our friends and mentors, thank you for your guidance and inspiration. Your wisdom and insights have shaped the ideas and concepts within these pages, and we are grateful for the valuable conversations and discussions we have shared.

A special thank you to the team at our publisher who believed in this project and provided the necessary resources and expertise to make it a reality. Your dedication and professionalism have been truly commendable.

We would also like to express our gratitude to the readers who have embraced this book. Your enthusiasm and support have been the driving force behind our efforts, and we hope that the knowledge and strategies shared within these pages have made a positive impact on your financial journey.

Lastly, we extend our appreciation to all the individuals who have contributed their time, insights, and expertise to this book. Your valuable input and collaboration have enriched the content and made it stronger.

Writing this book has been an incredible journey, and we are honored to have had the opportunity to share our knowledge and experiences with you. It is our sincere hope that "How to Make Money Without Money" serves as a source of inspiration, empowerment, and practical guidance as you embark on your own path towards financial freedom.

Thank you all for being a part of this transformative project.

With gratitude,

Sharon Larson.

About the Author

Sharon Larson (born 17 May, 1988) is an Australian acclaimed author known for her ability to engage readers on a profound level, she's the founder of Just Write Group.

Born and raised in the picturesque region of Yarra Valley, she found solace and inspiration in the power of words. As a child, Sharon would often spend hours lost in the pages of her favorite books, fueling her desire to create stories of her own.

Sharon Larson obtained her Bachelor's degree in Literature from the prestigious University of Melbourne. During her undergraduate studies, she delved into classic and contemporary works of literature, analyzing their themes, narratives, and writing techniques. This foundation in literature provided her with a deep appreciation for the power of storytelling and ignited her desire to create her own imaginative worlds.

After completing her education, Sharon embarked on a quest to bring her imagination to life through writing. She explored various genres, experimenting with different styles and themes. Her early works garnered critical acclaim within literary circles, catching the attention of both readers and publishers alike.

Sharon's educational journey played a crucial role in shaping her unique perspective and honing her writing skills. Known for her insatiable thirst for knowledge, she pursued a diverse range of academic disciplines that enriched her storytelling abilities.

Her keen observations and meticulous research form the foundation of her work, allowing her to present nuanced arguments and fresh perspectives.

Whether she is delving into historical events, analyzing social phenomena, or examining philosophical concepts, Sharon's prose is meticulously crafted to capture the essence of her subjects. Sharon's writing encourages readers to question their assumptions, challenge their beliefs, and embrace a spirit of intellectual curiosity.

Sharon Larson's life is not only marked by her literary accomplishments but also by a deep and enduring love that has influenced her work and brought joy to her personal journey. She shares a profound and inspiring marriage with her partner, Alexander Bennett, a renowned painter blessed with two daughters Mia and Emily.

COPYRIGHT

©2023 Sharon Larson | Just Write Group

All rights reserved. No part of this book may be reproduced in any form or by any electronic or mechanical means, including information storage and retrieval systems without the permission in writing from its author.
Except in the case of brief quotations embodied in critical reviews and certain other noncommercial uses permitted by copyright law.

For permissions requests or inquiries, please contact MeetMe@SharonLarson.com

Book Description:

Profit Power: Understanding the Art of Making Money

Unlock the secrets to financial success and harness the Profit Power within you. In this insightful and comprehensive guide, you will embark on a transformative journey that will revolutionize your understanding of wealth creation.

Profit Power: Understanding the Art of Making Money delves deep into the mindset, strategies, and principles that drive profitable ventures. Whether you're an aspiring entrepreneur, a seasoned business owner, or simply someone seeking to enhance your financial acumen, this book provides invaluable insights and practical advice to help you achieve your financial goals.

With a focus on empowering readers with knowledge and actionable steps, Profit Power covers a wide range of essential topics. You'll learn the psychology of success, how to overcome limiting beliefs, and develop a wealth consciousness that attracts prosperity into your life. Discover the fundamental principles of profit, differentiate between revenue and profit, and gain the skills to identify lucrative opportunities.

Financial literacy is a cornerstone of wealth creation, and this book equips you with the necessary tools. From mastering basic financial concepts to building effective marketing and sales strategies, you'll gain the knowledge to make informed decisions and optimize your profitability. Learn how to manage your finances, control costs, and maximize margins to ensure sustainable growth.

Profit Power also explores the world of investing, guiding you through the process of developing an investment strategy, diversifying your portfolio, and managing risks effectively. Additionally, it examines the role of technology in driving profit, providing insights on digital transformation, data analytics, and leveraging technology to streamline operations.

Economic cycles and trends can have a profound impact on financial success. This book offers strategies for navigating and thriving in challenging times, helping you adapt to market dynamics and capitalize on emerging trends. Furthermore, it emphasizes the importance of building long-term financial security, planning for the future, and leaving a lasting legacy through philanthropy and social impact.

Written in an accessible style, Profit Power combines real-world examples, practical tips, and expert guidance to empower you with the knowledge and mindset necessary to unlock your profit potential. Whether you're an entrepreneur, business leader, or someone seeking to enhance your financial well-being, this book will provide the essential tools to understand and master the art of making money.

Prepare to unleash your Profit Power and embark on a journey towards financial abundance and success.

Introduction: Unlocking the Profit Power

Welcome to "Profit Power: Understanding the Art of Making Money." In a world driven by commerce and fueled by aspirations, the pursuit of financial success is a universal endeavor. Whether you are an aspiring entrepreneur, a seasoned business professional, or simply someone seeking to improve your financial situation, this book is your guide to unlocking the secrets of profit.

In the pages that follow, we will explore the intricate and fascinating world of wealth creation. We will delve into the mindset, strategies, and principles that underpin the art of making money. Profit power is not just about accumulating wealth; it is about understanding the dynamics of profitability, uncovering opportunities, and harnessing the forces that drive financial success.

This book aims to equip you with the knowledge and tools necessary to navigate the complex terrain of profit generation. It is designed to help you develop a wealth consciousness, cultivate the right mindset, and make informed decisions that will propel you toward your financial goals.

Throughout this journey, we will examine various aspects of profit creation, from the fundamentals of economics and the power of financial literacy to the intricacies of building a profitable business and leveraging technology for success. We will explore the art of marketing and sales, managing finances for profitability, and the importance of investing wisely. Additionally, we will address the challenges of economic cycles and trends and guide you in building long-term wealth and leaving a lasting legacy.

This book is not a get-rich-quick scheme. It is a comprehensive exploration of the principles and strategies that have stood the test of time, providing a solid foundation for those who are committed to achieving financial success. It will require your attention, active engagement, and willingness to apply the lessons learned. By doing so, you will gain the insights necessary to unlock your profit power and navigate the ever-changing landscape of wealth creation.

Whether you are an aspiring entrepreneur with a groundbreaking idea, a business owner seeking to maximize profits, or an individual looking to enhance your financial well-being, "Profit Power: Understanding the Art of Making Money" will serve as your compass on this transformative journey. Together, let us embark on this exploration of profit power and discover the art of making money.

Chapter 1: The Mindset of Wealth

Welcome to Chapter 1 of our comprehensive guide on achieving wealth and financial success. In this chapter, we delve into the foundational aspect of wealth creation—the mindset. Before we explore the practical strategies and techniques that can lead to financial prosperity, it is crucial to understand that true wealth begins within oneself.

Wealth is not solely determined by external factors such as income or material possessions; rather, it is a state of mind, a set of beliefs, attitudes, and habits that shape our relationship with money and opportunities. Developing the mindset of wealth is the first step towards unlocking your potential for abundance and prosperity.

In this chapter, we will explore the key elements of the mindset of wealth and how it can influence your financial journey. We will delve into the importance of self-belief, positive thinking, and a growth mindset in building a strong foundation for wealth creation. We will also examine the role of goal-setting, perseverance, and resilience in overcoming obstacles and achieving long-term success.

Moreover, we will address the limiting beliefs and self-sabotaging behaviors that can hinder your progress towards wealth. By identifying and challenging these roadblocks, you can reframe your mindset and develop new empowering beliefs that align with your financial goals.

Throughout this chapter, we will provide practical exercises and insights to help you cultivate a mindset that embraces abundance, opportunity, and financial freedom. By adopting the mindset of wealth, you can transform your relationship with money and pave the way for a more prosperous future.

Remember, wealth is not an end in itself but rather a means to live a life of fulfillment, security, and the ability to make a positive impact. So, let us embark on this journey together and lay the groundwork for a mindset that will set you on the path to financial prosperity.

1.1 The Power of a Wealth Consciousness

Introduction:
In our quest to understand the art of making money, it is essential to begin by exploring the power of a wealth consciousness. Our mindset and beliefs play a significant role in shaping our financial reality. By adopting a mindset that aligns with abundance and prosperity, we open ourselves to limitless possibilities and unlock the true potential of our profit power.

Key Concepts:
1. Shifting from Scarcity to Abundance: Understanding that the world is abundant and that there are ample opportunities for financial success is a fundamental shift in mindset. Letting go of scarcity thinking and embracing abundance allows us to see opportunities where others see obstacles.

2. The Law of Attraction: The law of attraction states that like attracts like. By focusing on positive thoughts, visualizing success, and aligning our energy with our financial goals, we can attract the resources, people, and opportunities needed to achieve them.

3. Overcoming Limiting Beliefs: Many of us harbor limiting beliefs about money and wealth, often inherited from our upbringing or societal conditioning. Recognizing and challenging these beliefs is crucial for developing a wealth consciousness. By reframing our beliefs and adopting empowering money mindsets, we can break free from self-imposed limitations and create a new financial reality.

Strategies for Cultivating a Wealth Consciousness:
a) Mindfulness and Self-Awareness: Developing a wealth consciousness begins with self-awareness. Paying attention to our thoughts, emotions, and beliefs about money allows us to identify any negative patterns or limiting beliefs that may be holding us back.

b) Affirmations and Visualization: Affirmations are positive statements that reinforce our desired financial outcomes. By repeating affirmations regularly and visualizing ourselves already achieving our goals, we strengthen our belief in our ability to create wealth.

c) Surrounding Yourself with Positive Influences: The company we keep significantly impacts our mindset. Surrounding ourselves with individuals who have a wealth consciousness and who inspire us to achieve financial success can be highly motivating and supportive.

d) Continuous Learning and Personal Growth: Adopting a wealth consciousness is an ongoing journey of learning and personal growth. Continuously educating ourselves about finance, investing, and wealth-building strategies expands our knowledge base and empowers us to make informed decisions.

Conclusion:
Cultivating a wealth consciousness is a crucial first step in harnessing the profit power within us. By shifting our mindset from scarcity to abundance, embracing the law of attraction, and overcoming limiting beliefs, we lay the groundwork for attracting financial success. With mindfulness, affirmations, positive influences, and a commitment to continuous learning, we empower ourselves to

create a life of wealth and abundance. Remember, the power to shape your financial destiny lies within your mindset.

Chapter 1.2: Developing a Wealth Consciousness

Introduction:
In the pursuit of financial success, one of the most crucial aspects is developing a wealth consciousness. Your mindset plays a pivotal role in shaping your attitudes, beliefs, and actions towards money and abundance. In this chapter, we will explore the key principles and strategies for cultivating a mindset that aligns with your financial goals and empowers you to unlock your full potential.

1. The Power of Beliefs:
    1.1 Understanding the influence of beliefs on financial outcomes
    1.2 Identifying and challenging limiting beliefs
    1.3 Cultivating empowering beliefs for wealth creation

2. Shifting Your Money Paradigm:
    2.1 Examining your current money mindset
    2.2 Recognizing and releasing scarcity thinking
    2.3 Embracing an abundance mentality

3. Visualization and Affirmations:
    3.1 Harnessing the power of visualization for financial success

3.2 Creating affirmations that reinforce abundance and prosperity

3.3 Incorporating daily practices to reinforce positive beliefs

4. Surrounding Yourself with Positive Influences:
   4.1 The impact of your social environment on your mindset
   4.2 Building a supportive network of like-minded individuals
   4.3 Seeking mentors and role models for inspiration and guidance

5. Embracing Gratitude and Appreciation:
   5.1 Cultivating a mindset of gratitude for current and future wealth
   5.2 Practicing appreciation for financial blessings and opportunities
   5.3 Incorporating gratitude rituals into your daily life

6. Overcoming Fear and Taking Calculated Risks:
   6.1 Understanding the role of fear in hindering financial success
   6.2 Developing strategies to overcome fear and embrace risk
   6.3 Learning from failures and using setbacks as stepping stones to growth

7. Aligning Actions with Intentions:
   7.1 Setting clear financial goals and intentions

7.2 Creating an action plan to manifest your desired outcomes

7.3 Maintaining consistency and discipline in your financial pursuits

Conclusion:
Cultivating a wealth consciousness is a transformative journey that has the potential to revolutionize your relationship with money and unlock new opportunities for financial success. By embracing empowering beliefs, shifting your money paradigm, practicing visualization and affirmations, surrounding yourself with positive influences, expressing gratitude, and taking calculated risks, you can create a mindset that aligns with abundance and prosperity. Remember, your thoughts and beliefs shape your reality, so choose to cultivate a wealth consciousness that supports your financial goals and empowers you to live a life of abundance.

Chapter 1.3: Overcoming Limiting Beliefs

Introduction:
In our pursuit of financial success, it is essential to recognize and address the presence of limiting beliefs that can hinder our progress. Limiting beliefs are deeply ingrained thoughts and perceptions that hold us back from reaching our full potential. In this chapter, we will explore the power of overcoming these limiting beliefs and how to cultivate a mindset of abundance and possibility.

1. Understanding Limiting Beliefs:
   1.1 Definition and Impact: We delve into the concept of limiting beliefs, explaining how they are formed and the negative impact they can have on our financial aspirations.
   1.2 Common Types of Limiting Beliefs: Explore some of the most common limiting beliefs related to money, success, and wealth accumulation that can hinder our progress.
   1.3 Recognizing Personal Limiting Beliefs: Learn how to identify and become aware of your own limiting beliefs by examining your thoughts, emotions, and patterns of behavior.

2. Challenging and Reframing Limiting Beliefs:
   2.1 Questioning the Validity: Understand the importance of critically evaluating your limiting beliefs and questioning their validity by seeking evidence to the contrary.
   2.2 Changing Your Narrative: Discover techniques and strategies to reframe your limiting beliefs into empowering beliefs that support your financial goals and aspirations.
   2.3 Affirmations and Visualization: Learn how to use positive affirmations and visualization exercises to reprogram your subconscious mind and reinforce new empowering beliefs.

3. Embracing a Growth Mindset:
   3.1 Cultivating a Growth Mindset: Understand the concept of a growth mindset and its importance in

overcoming limiting beliefs. Explore ways to develop and nurture a growth mindset to support your financial journey.

3.2 Embracing Failure and Learning: Learn how to reframe failure as an opportunity for growth and learning, allowing you to embrace challenges and setbacks as valuable stepping stones towards success.

3.3 Seeking Support and Surrounding Yourself with Positivity: Discover the significance of surrounding yourself with a supportive network of like-minded individuals who can uplift and inspire you on your path to financial success.

4. Taking Action and Building Momentum:

4.1 Setting Realistic Goals: Learn how to set clear, realistic goals that align with your vision and values, providing a sense of purpose and direction in your financial journey.

4.2 Taking Small Steps and Celebrating Progress: Explore the power of taking consistent, incremental actions towards your goals, and celebrate your achievements along the way to maintain motivation and momentum.

4.3 Embracing Continuous Growth: Understand that overcoming limiting beliefs is an ongoing process, and commit to continuous personal growth and development to expand your mindset and maximize your potential.

Conclusion:

In this chapter, we have explored the significance of overcoming limiting beliefs on our path to financial success. By recognizing and challenging these beliefs, reframing them into empowering narratives, and cultivating a growth mindset, we pave the way for greater abundance and achievement. Remember, your beliefs shape your reality, and by embracing a mindset of possibility and taking consistent action, you can break free from limitations and unlock your full potential for financial prosperity.

Introduction to Chapter 2: The Fundamentals of Profit

In our pursuit of financial success and wealth creation, it is essential to understand the core principles and fundamental concepts that drive profitability. Chapter 2, "The Fundamentals of Profit," delves into the essential elements that underpin a prosperous venture or investment. By grasping these principles and incorporating them into your financial endeavors, you can significantly enhance your chances of achieving sustainable profitability.

This chapter serves as a comprehensive guide to equip you with the necessary knowledge and insights to navigate the intricate landscape of profit generation. We will explore the various factors that contribute to profitability, ranging from cost management and revenue optimization to risk assessment and market dynamics. By gaining a deep understanding of these fundamentals, you will be better prepared to make informed decisions and take strategic actions that yield financial gains.

Throughout this chapter, we will examine real-life case studies, industry best practices, and proven strategies employed by successful entrepreneurs and investors. By drawing on these experiences, you can uncover valuable lessons and practical techniques that can be applied to your own financial pursuits.

Whether you are a business owner aiming to improve your company's bottom line, an aspiring entrepreneur seeking to launch a profitable venture, or an investor looking to maximize returns, this chapter will provide you with the tools and insights to lay a solid foundation for sustained profitability.

As you delve into "The Fundamentals of Profit," keep an open mind, embrace a growth mindset, and remain committed to applying the principles outlined in this chapter. Remember, profitability is not a singular event but an ongoing process that requires continuous learning, adaptation, and refinement. By mastering these fundamentals, you will be well on your way to achieving financial success and realizing your wealth creation goals.

2.1 The Psychology of Profit: Unleashing Your Money Mindset

In the pursuit of profit, understanding the psychology behind our relationship with money is paramount. Our beliefs, attitudes, and emotions play a significant role in shaping our financial decisions and outcomes. In this section, we explore the psychology of profit and delve into the key factors that influence our money mindset.

To begin, we examine the impact of our beliefs about money. Deeply ingrained beliefs about wealth and abundance, often formed in childhood, can either empower or limit our financial success. It is crucial to identify and challenge any negative beliefs or scarcity mindsets that may hinder our ability to create and attract wealth. By adopting a mindset of abundance, we open ourselves to new opportunities and possibilities.

Emotions also play a pivotal role in our financial decision-making. Fear, greed, and impatience can lead to irrational choices that undermine profitability. Learning to manage emotions and make rational, objective decisions is essential for long-term financial success. We explore techniques for emotional intelligence and self-awareness, enabling you to navigate the ups and downs of the financial landscape with clarity and composure.

Furthermore, we delve into the concept of risk tolerance and its influence on profit-seeking. Each individual has a unique risk tolerance level, which affects their willingness to undertake financial risks. We examine strategies for assessing and managing risk, allowing you to strike a balance between prudence and the pursuit of profitable ventures.

Additionally, we explore the power of visualization and positive affirmations in shaping our money mindset. By vividly envisioning our financial goals and consistently affirming our ability to achieve them, we align our subconscious mind with our conscious desires. This alignment strengthens our belief in our capacity to make money and attracts opportunities that align with our aspirations.

Lastly, we discuss the importance of continuous personal growth and financial education. As we expand our knowledge and skills, we enhance our confidence and adaptability in the ever-changing landscape of profit-making. We explore various resources and strategies for lifelong learning, encouraging you to invest in your personal and financial development.

By understanding and harnessing the psychology of profit, you unlock the ability to make sound financial decisions, attract wealth, and overcome self-imposed limitations. Through introspection, emotional mastery, risk assessment, visualization, and ongoing education, you lay the foundation for a powerful money mindset that propels you towards sustained profitability.

Remember, profit is not solely a product of external circumstances but is profoundly influenced by our internal beliefs, attitudes, and behaviors. By mastering the psychology of profit, you tap into the immense power within you to create and maximize your financial success.

2.2 Profit vs. Revenue: Understanding the Difference

In the pursuit of financial success, it is crucial to understand the fundamental distinction between profit and revenue. While the two terms are often used interchangeably, they represent distinct aspects of a business's financial performance. By comprehending their differences, you can gain a clearer perspective on your company's financial health and make informed decisions to maximize profitability.

Revenue, also known as sales or turnover, refers to the total amount of money generated from the sale of goods or services during a specific period. It represents the inflow of funds into the business resulting from its primary operations. Revenue is a critical metric that demonstrates the overall demand for your products or services and serves as a measure of your business's top-line performance.

Profit, on the other hand, is the financial gain that remains after deducting all expenses incurred in the production, operation, and distribution of goods or services. It is the surplus that remains when revenue exceeds the costs associated with running the business. Profit is a key indicator of a company's profitability and its ability to generate returns for its owners and investors.

While revenue provides an important snapshot of a company's sales volume, profit is a more comprehensive measure of financial success. Profit takes into account not only the inflow of funds but also the outflow of expenses, including cost of goods sold, operating expenses, taxes, and other overheads. It reflects the true financial viability of a business and its capacity to generate sustainable returns.

Understanding the relationship between revenue and profit is essential for effective financial management. A business can experience high revenue figures but still struggle to achieve profitability if expenses outweigh the incoming funds. By analyzing the profit margin, which is the ratio of profit to revenue, you can assess the efficiency of your operations and identify areas for improvement.

Moreover, focusing solely on revenue growth without considering profitability can be misleading. A business may experience rapid revenue expansion, but if profit margins are thin or nonexistent, it may face financial instability and struggle to sustain its operations in the long run. Profitability is crucial for reinvesting in the business, expanding operations, and achieving sustained growth.

In summary, revenue and profit are distinct concepts that require careful consideration in financial analysis. Revenue represents the total sales generated, while profit represents the surplus after deducting all expenses. By recognizing the difference between these two metrics and prioritizing profitability, you can make strategic decisions that drive your business towards sustainable financial success.

2.3 Identifying Profitable Opportunities

In the pursuit of financial success, one of the key skills you must develop is the ability to identify profitable opportunities. Opportunities for profit exist in various forms, ranging from entrepreneurial ventures to investment prospects. By honing your discernment and understanding the factors that contribute to profitability, you can make informed decisions that maximize your chances of success.

To identify profitable opportunities, it is crucial to conduct thorough market research and analysis. This involves studying market trends, assessing consumer demands, and identifying gaps or inefficiencies that present opportunities for growth. By staying attuned to the needs and desires of your target audience, you can tailor your products or services to meet their demands effectively.

Furthermore, understanding the competitive landscape is essential. Analyze your competitors' strengths and weaknesses, evaluate their market positioning, and identify areas where you can differentiate yourself and offer unique value. Differentiation can be a powerful tool in capturing a share of the market and generating sustainable profits.

In addition to external factors, it is crucial to assess your own strengths, skills, and resources. Evaluate your expertise, experience, and interests to identify areas where you can leverage your advantages and create a competitive edge. By aligning your passions and capabilities with profitable opportunities, you increase the likelihood of long-term success and fulfillment.

Risk assessment is another critical aspect of identifying profitable opportunities. Every venture carries a degree of risk, and it is important to assess and manage these risks effectively. Conduct a thorough analysis of the potential risks involved, including market volatility, financial constraints, and operational challenges. Develop contingency plans and mitigation strategies to minimize potential setbacks and protect your profitability.

Moreover, staying informed about emerging technologies, industry trends, and regulatory changes can help you spot new opportunities before others do. Maintain a curious and adaptive mindset, continuously seeking knowledge and staying abreast of relevant developments. This proactive approach can enable you to capitalize on emerging trends and seize opportunities as they arise.

Lastly, it is crucial to evaluate the potential return on investment (ROI) and profitability of each opportunity. Consider the financial factors such as revenue potential, cost structure, scalability, and expected growth. Conduct thorough financial analysis, including forecasting and sensitivity analysis, to assess the viability and profitability of the opportunity.

Remember, identifying profitable opportunities requires a combination of research, analysis, self-awareness, and risk assessment. It is an ongoing process that requires continuous learning and adaptation. By mastering this skill, you empower yourself to make informed decisions that align with your financial goals and pave the way for long-term profitability.

Chapter 3: The Power of Financial Literacy

Introduction:

In today's fast-paced and ever-changing world, financial literacy is not just an option; it's an absolute necessity. The ability to understand and manage your finances effectively can mean the difference between a life of financial struggle and one of abundance and prosperity. Yet, despite its importance, financial literacy remains a topic that is often overlooked or misunderstood.

In this chapter, we delve deep into the power of financial literacy and its profound impact on your wealth-building journey. We will explore how developing a solid foundation of financial knowledge can empower you to make informed decisions, seize opportunities, and navigate the complex landscape of money with confidence.

Financial literacy encompasses a wide range of essential concepts and skills. It involves understanding basic financial principles, such as budgeting, saving, and debt management. It also entails comprehending more complex topics like investing, risk assessment, and asset allocation. By equipping yourself with these vital skills, you can unlock the door to financial freedom and create a secure future for yourself and your loved ones.

Throughout this chapter, we will guide you on a transformative journey, unveiling the key aspects of financial literacy and providing practical strategies for implementation. We will explore the mindset required to develop a strong financial foundation, the tools and resources available for expanding your knowledge, and the importance of continuous learning in an ever-evolving financial landscape.

Moreover, we will emphasize the significance of taking control of your financial destiny. We live in a world where financial decisions are constantly bombarding us, whether it's choosing between different types of loans, managing credit card debt, or deciphering investment opportunities. With financial literacy as your compass, you will be empowered to make educated choices, ensuring that your hard-earned money is working for you, rather than the other way around.

Remember, financial literacy is not an exclusive club reserved for a select few. It is a skill set that can be cultivated and honed over time. Regardless of your current level of financial knowledge, this chapter will provide you with the tools, insights, and strategies to enhance your financial literacy and transform your relationship with money.

So, let us embark on this enlightening journey together. By delving into the power of financial literacy, you are taking a crucial step towards unlocking your full wealth-building potential. Prepare to expand your horizons, empower your decision-making, and discover the path to financial success. The power is in your hands; it's time to seize it.

3.1 The Importance of Financial Education

In today's complex and ever-changing financial landscape, possessing a solid foundation of financial literacy is crucial for anyone seeking to harness the profit power. Financial education empowers individuals to make informed decisions, manage their resources effectively, and navigate the intricate world of money with confidence.

In this section, we will explore the importance of financial education and its profound impact on personal and business finances. We will delve into the benefits of acquiring financial knowledge, discuss the consequences of financial illiteracy, and provide practical steps to enhance your financial literacy.

Why is financial education important? It equips you with the necessary skills to make sound financial decisions, including budgeting, investing, and managing debt. By understanding concepts such as compound interest, inflation, and risk management, you can make informed choices that align with your financial goals.

Financial education also fosters a sense of empowerment and control over your financial well-being. It enables you to take charge of your financial future, rather than being at the mercy of circumstances or relying solely on the advice of others. With a solid understanding of financial principles, you become a more active participant in financial matters and can better advocate for your own interests.

Moreover, financial education helps protect you from falling victim to scams, fraud, and predatory financial practices. By being knowledgeable about financial concepts and regulations, you can identify warning signs and make informed decisions that safeguard your assets and financial security.

Unfortunately, the consequences of financial illiteracy can be severe. Without the necessary knowledge and skills, individuals may struggle with debt, make poor investment choices, or fall prey to financial pitfalls. Lack of financial literacy can perpetuate a cycle of poverty and hinder economic growth, both on an individual and societal level.

To enhance your financial literacy, consider the following steps:

1. Seek out educational resources: Take advantage of books, online courses, workshops, and seminars focused on personal finance and investment. Many reputable organizations and institutions offer free or low-cost resources to help you develop your financial acumen.

2. Engage with financial professionals: Consult with financial advisors, accountants, or investment experts to gain insights tailored to your specific circumstances. They can provide personalized guidance and help you understand complex financial concepts.

3. Stay informed: Keep up with financial news, market trends, and economic indicators. Subscribe to reputable financial publications or follow trusted financial websites to stay abreast of developments that may impact your financial decisions.

4. Practice financial discipline: Apply the knowledge you acquire by practicing responsible financial habits. Create a budget, save diligently, and make informed choices when it comes to spending, borrowing, and investing.

By investing in your financial education, you lay the groundwork for financial success. The power of financial literacy extends far beyond mere numbers and transactions; it empowers you to shape your financial destiny, seize opportunities, and build a prosperous future.

In the following sections of this chapter, we will explore the fundamental concepts and skills that form the bedrock of financial literacy. With each step, you will gain a deeper understanding of the financial world and be better equipped to make decisions that maximize your profit potential.

3.2 Mastering Basic Financial Concepts

In the previous section, we discussed the importance of financial education as a key component of achieving financial success. Now, let's delve deeper into mastering basic financial concepts that will empower you to make informed decisions and take control of your financial well-being.

1. Budgeting: Budgeting is the foundation of sound financial management. Learn how to create a budget that aligns with your income and expenses, allowing you to allocate funds wisely and prioritize your financial goals. Understand the importance of tracking your spending and making adjustments when necessary to stay on track.

2. Saving and Investing: Explore the principles of saving and investing to build wealth over time. Discover the various types of savings accounts, investment vehicles, and their associated risks and returns. Learn about the power of compounding and how to leverage it to grow your wealth.

Develop a savings and investment strategy that aligns with your financial goals and risk tolerance.

3. Debt Management: Understand the implications of debt and develop effective strategies for managing it. Learn about different types of debt, such as credit card debt, student loans, and mortgages, and explore strategies for debt repayment, consolidation, and avoiding excessive interest payments. Gain insights into credit scores and how they impact your financial well-being.

4. Insurance and Risk Management: Familiarize yourself with the concept of insurance and its role in protecting your assets and mitigating financial risks. Learn about different types of insurance, such as health insurance, life insurance, and property insurance, and evaluate your insurance needs based on your personal circumstances.

5. Retirement Planning: Start planning for your future by understanding the importance of retirement savings. Learn about different retirement accounts, such as 401(k)s and IRAs, and explore strategies to maximize your contributions and take advantage of employer matching programs. Gain insights into retirement planning calculators and the concept of retirement income replacement.

6. Taxation: Develop a basic understanding of tax principles and how they affect your financial decisions. Learn about different types of taxes,

such as income tax, capital gains tax, and sales tax, and explore strategies for tax optimization, such as deductions, credits, and tax-efficient investment strategies. Consult a tax professional for personalized advice.

By mastering these basic financial concepts, you will gain the knowledge and skills needed to navigate the financial landscape with confidence. Remember, financial literacy is an ongoing process, and it's important to stay informed and adapt to changing economic conditions. With a solid understanding of these fundamental concepts, you will be well-equipped to make informed financial decisions, build wealth, and secure a brighter financial future.

3.3 Essential Skills for Financial Success

In Chapter 3, we have emphasized the importance of financial literacy in your journey towards financial success. While having a solid understanding of basic financial concepts is crucial, it is equally important to develop and hone specific skills that will empower you to make sound financial decisions and effectively manage your money. In this section, we will explore three essential skills that will enhance your financial prowess.

1. Budgeting and Financial Planning:

One of the fundamental skills for financial success is budgeting and financial planning. Creating a budget allows you to track your income and expenses, prioritize your spending, and allocate funds towards your goals. Learn how to set realistic financial goals, create a budgeting framework, and monitor your progress regularly. With strong budgeting skills, you can make informed choices, control your spending, and build a solid foundation for your financial future.

2. Debt Management:

Debt can be a significant obstacle on your path to financial success. Developing effective debt management skills is essential for maintaining a healthy financial status. Understand different types of debt, such as credit cards, loans, and mortgages, and learn how to manage them responsibly. Explore strategies to reduce and eliminate debt, prioritize repayment plans, and negotiate favorable terms. By mastering debt management, you can minimize financial stress, improve your credit score, and create opportunities for future investments.

3. Risk Assessment and Risk Management:

Financial success involves an element of risk-taking, but it is essential to approach risk with caution and a calculated mindset. Developing the skill of risk assessment and risk management will help you evaluate potential risks associated with your financial decisions and take appropriate steps to mitigate them. Understand different types of financial risks, such as market volatility, investment risks, and unforeseen events, and explore strategies to diversify your portfolio, establish emergency funds, and protect your assets. By effectively managing risks, you can safeguard your financial well-being and make more informed choices.

By focusing on these essential skills for financial success—budgeting and financial planning, debt management, and risk assessment and management—you will enhance your financial literacy and empower yourself to make sound financial decisions. Remember that mastering these skills takes practice and continuous learning. Embrace the opportunity to strengthen your financial acumen and apply these skills in your daily life. With time and dedication, you will navigate the complexities of personal finance with confidence and achieve your financial goals.

Continue your journey into the world of profit power as we move forward to explore the strategies and principles of building a profitable business in Chapter 4.

Chapter 4: Building a Profitable Business - Introduction

Welcome to Chapter 4 of our book, where we delve into the exciting world of building a profitable business. In this chapter, we will explore the key principles, strategies, and practices that can transform your entrepreneurial dreams into a thriving enterprise.

Starting and running a business is an exhilarating endeavor, filled with opportunities and challenges. It requires vision, determination, and a deep understanding of the fundamental aspects that drive profitability. Whether you are an aspiring entrepreneur or an existing business owner looking to enhance your profitability, this chapter will provide you with valuable insights and actionable steps to achieve your goals.

Building a profitable business begins with a solid foundation. We will discuss the importance of defining your business mission and values, as well as how to develop a compelling business plan that outlines your goals, target market, competitive advantage, and financial projections.
Understanding your market and identifying your customers' needs and desires are critical elements

in creating a business that not only survives but thrives in a competitive landscape.

Next, we will explore the vital components of effective operations management. From optimizing your supply chain to streamlining your processes, we will guide you in maximizing efficiency and minimizing costs. We will also delve into the significance of creating a customer-centric culture, fostering innovation, and building a strong team that shares your vision and values.

Marketing and sales strategies play a crucial role in driving business growth and profitability. We will explore various marketing channels, both traditional and digital, and discuss how to craft compelling messages that resonate with your target audience. From identifying the right marketing mix to leveraging social media and content marketing, we will equip you with the tools to effectively promote your products or services and attract loyal customers.

Additionally, we will delve into financial management practices that are essential for sustaining and expanding your business. From budgeting and cash flow management to pricing strategies and profit optimization, we will provide you with the knowledge and techniques to make sound financial decisions and drive profitability.

Throughout this chapter, we will showcase real-life examples and case studies of successful businesses that have achieved remarkable profitability. By learning from their experiences and applying the principles and strategies shared in this chapter, you will be well-equipped to build a thriving and profitable business of your own.

Remember, building a profitable business requires perseverance, adaptability, and a willingness to continuously learn and evolve. So, let's embark on this exciting journey together and unlock the secrets to building a business that not only generates profits but also creates long-term value for your customers and stakeholders.

Chapter 4: Building a Profitable Business

4.1 Choosing the Right Business Model

The foundation of a profitable business lies in choosing the right business model. A business model serves as the blueprint for how your organization creates, delivers, and captures value. It defines the core aspects of your business, such as your target market, products or services, revenue streams, and cost structure.

In this section, we will explore the critical factors to consider when selecting a business model that aligns with your goals and maximizes your profit potential. Here are some key points to contemplate:

1. Understanding your market: Start by conducting thorough market research to gain insights into your target audience, their needs, and existing market dynamics. Identify any gaps or opportunities that can be leveraged to your advantage.

2. Value proposition: Define a compelling value proposition that sets your business apart from competitors. Clearly articulate the unique value you offer to customers and how it solves their problems or fulfills their desires.

3. Revenue streams: Determine the most effective revenue streams for your business. Will you generate income through product sales, service fees, subscriptions, licensing, or a combination of these? Assess the profitability and scalability of each revenue stream option.

4. Cost structure: Analyze the costs involved in running your business. Consider factors such as production or acquisition costs, operational expenses, marketing and advertising costs, and overhead expenses. Strive to optimize your cost structure to maximize profitability without compromising quality.

5. Scalability and growth potential: Assess the scalability and growth potential of your chosen business model. Can it be easily replicated or expanded to reach new markets or customer

segments? Consider the long-term sustainability and profitability of your business model as it evolves over time.

6. Competitive advantage: Identify your competitive advantage within the market. This could be based on factors such as pricing, quality, innovation, customer service, or distribution channels. Leverage your unique strengths to position yourself as the preferred choice among customers.

7. Flexibility and adaptability: In today's rapidly changing business landscape, flexibility and adaptability are essential. Choose a business model that allows for agility and quick adjustments to meet evolving customer needs and market conditions.

Remember, choosing the right business model is a strategic decision that can significantly impact your profitability. Take the time to thoroughly evaluate your options, consider various scenarios, and seek expert advice if needed. A well-designed business model sets the stage for long-term success and profitability by aligning your operations with market demand and creating sustainable value for your customers.

Chapter 4.2: Market Research and Analysis

In the pursuit of building a profitable business, one of the essential steps is conducting thorough market research and analysis. Understanding the market landscape and your target audience is crucial for developing a winning business strategy and positioning your offerings for success.

Market research involves gathering and analyzing information about your industry, competitors, customers, and broader market trends. By gaining insights into these key areas, you can make informed decisions and tailor your products or services to meet the needs and preferences of your target market. Here are some key aspects to consider in market research and analysis:

1. Identifying your target market: Clearly defining your target audience is vital for effective marketing and sales efforts. Research their demographics, psychographics, behaviors, and preferences. Understand their pain points, desires, and motivations. This knowledge will enable you to create compelling marketing messages and develop products or services that truly resonate with your customers.

2. Analyzing competition: Thoroughly study your competitors to identify their strengths, weaknesses, and market positioning. Analyze their product offerings, pricing strategies, marketing tactics, and customer feedback. This analysis will help you differentiate your business and identify areas where you can outperform the competition.

3. Assessing market size and trends: Determine the size and growth potential of your target market. Analyze industry reports, market research studies, and economic indicators to understand the market dynamics, trends, and opportunities. This analysis will help you identify niches, untapped markets, and emerging trends that you can capitalize on.

4. Conducting customer surveys and feedback: Engage directly with your potential customers through surveys, interviews, or focus groups. Gather feedback on their preferences, pain points, and expectations. This qualitative data will provide valuable insights into customer needs and preferences, helping you refine your offerings and improve customer satisfaction.

5. Evaluating pricing and value proposition: Determine the optimal pricing strategy for your products or services based on market demand, competitor pricing, and perceived value. Understand what features, benefits, or unique selling propositions differentiate your offerings and how they align with customer expectations.

6. Monitoring industry and market trends: Stay abreast of the latest developments in your industry and broader market. Monitor technological advancements, regulatory changes, consumer trends, and competitive innovations. This awareness will help you identify opportunities and adapt your business strategy accordingly.

By investing time and effort in comprehensive market research and analysis, you lay a solid foundation for your business. The insights gained will inform your marketing, sales, and product development efforts, enabling you to position your business for long-term profitability and sustainable growth.

Remember, market research is an ongoing process. As your business evolves and market dynamics change, continue to gather data, analyze trends, and adapt your strategies accordingly. By staying attuned to your target market's needs and preferences, you can continuously refine your offerings and maintain a competitive edge in the ever-changing business landscape.

Chapter 4.3: Developing a Winning Value Proposition

In Chapter 4.2, we explored the importance of market research and analysis in building a profitable business. Now, let's dive deeper into the crucial aspect of developing a winning value proposition. Your value proposition is what sets you apart from your competitors and convinces customers that your product or service is the best choice for them.

1. Understanding Customer Needs: To create a compelling value proposition, you must have a

deep understanding of your target customers' needs, desires, and pain points. Conduct thorough market research, gather customer feedback, and analyze industry trends to gain insights into what your customers truly value.

2. Unique Selling Proposition (USP): Identify your unique selling proposition—a distinctive factor that sets your product or service apart from others in the market. It could be a specific feature, superior quality, exceptional customer service, or innovative technology. Highlight this USP in your value proposition to clearly communicate why customers should choose you over your competitors.

3. Benefits and Differentiation: Clearly articulate the benefits your product or service offers to customers. How does it solve their problems or fulfill their desires? Emphasize the unique value you provide and how it differentiates you from the competition. Focus on the outcomes and results customers can expect when they choose your offering.

4. Clear and Concise Messaging: Your value proposition should be communicated in a clear and concise manner. Avoid jargon or complex language that might confuse potential customers. Use simple, compelling language that clearly conveys the value you offer and resonates with your target audience.

5. Emotional Appeal: Don't underestimate the power of emotions in influencing purchasing decisions. Tap into the emotional aspect of your customers' needs and desires when crafting your value proposition. Appeal to their aspirations, desires for status or recognition, or their desire for convenience and peace of mind.

6. Test and Refine: Crafting an effective value proposition may require experimentation and refinement. Test different versions of your value proposition and gather feedback from customers to see what resonates most with them. Continuously monitor market dynamics and be willing to adjust your value proposition to stay relevant and competitive.

By developing a winning value proposition, you can effectively communicate the unique value you offer to your target customers. It helps you stand out in a crowded marketplace and influences customers to choose your product or service over alternatives. Invest time and effort into understanding your customers' needs and desires, defining your unique selling proposition, and crafting a compelling message that resonates with your audience. Remember, a well-crafted value proposition is a powerful tool in driving your business's profitability and long-term success.

Chapter 5: Effective Marketing and Sales Strategies

In today's competitive business landscape, the ability to effectively market and sell your products or services is crucial for achieving profitability and sustaining long-term success. Chapter 5 delves into the realm of marketing and sales, exploring the strategies and techniques that can propel your business to new heights.

This chapter recognizes that marketing and sales are not just isolated functions within a company but intertwined disciplines that work in harmony to drive revenue and growth. Whether you are a seasoned entrepreneur or a budding business owner, understanding the fundamentals of marketing and sales will empower you to reach your target audience, engage them effectively, and ultimately convert them into loyal customers.

Within these pages, you will explore a wide range of topics related to marketing and sales, starting with market research and analysis. Discover how to identify your target market, understand their needs and preferences, and position your offerings in a way that resonates with them. We will delve into the world of branding and messaging, uncovering the secrets to creating a strong brand identity and crafting compelling messages that captivate your audience.

Furthermore, this chapter will guide you through various marketing channels and strategies, exploring both traditional and digital methods. Learn how to develop a comprehensive marketing plan, utilizing tactics such as advertising, public relations, social media marketing, content marketing, and more. Delve into the world of search engine optimization (SEO) and discover how to optimize your online presence to increase visibility and attract organic traffic.

Equally important is the art of salesmanship, as this chapter will equip you with the essential skills to close deals and generate revenue. From effective communication techniques to understanding customer objections and providing persuasive solutions, you will gain insights into the psychology of selling and learn how to build strong relationships with your customers.

Moreover, this chapter emphasizes the importance of data-driven decision-making in marketing and sales. Discover how to measure and analyze key performance indicators (KPIs) to gauge the effectiveness of your strategies and make informed adjustments to optimize your results. By harnessing the power of analytics, you can refine your marketing campaigns, maximize your return on investment, and drive sustainable business growth.

In summary, Chapter 5 aims to equip you with the knowledge and tools necessary to create effective marketing and sales strategies that propel your business forward. With the right approach and a deep understanding of your target audience, you can build a strong brand, engage customers authentically, and drive profitability in a competitive marketplace. Let's dive in and explore the world of marketing and sales together, unlocking the potential to achieve remarkable success.

5.1 Understanding the Consumer Mindset

In the ever-evolving marketplace, understanding the consumer mindset is crucial for any business aiming to drive profitability. Consumer behavior is influenced by a variety of factors, including psychological, social, and cultural aspects. By gaining insights into how consumers think, feel, and make purchasing decisions, you can tailor your marketing strategies and offerings to meet their needs effectively.

This section will delve into the following key aspects of the consumer mindset:

1. Consumer Motivations: Explore the underlying motivations that drive consumers to make purchasing decisions. Uncover the importance of factors such as convenience, price, quality, status, and emotional satisfaction. By understanding these

motivations, you can align your products or services to fulfill consumers' desires and create compelling value propositions.

2. Decision-Making Processes: Learn about the various decision-making processes consumers go through when considering a purchase. Explore the differences between rational decision-making and emotional decision-making, and how these processes are influenced by external factors such as marketing messages, peer recommendations, and personal experiences. Understanding these processes allows you to craft persuasive marketing campaigns that resonate with your target audience.

3. Consumer Perception: Discover how consumers perceive and interpret information about products or services. Explore the concept of brand perception, including brand image, brand reputation, and brand loyalty. Understand the impact of advertising, packaging, and other sensory cues on consumers' perception and purchase decisions. By managing and shaping consumer perception, you can establish a strong brand identity and differentiate yourself from competitors.

4. Customer Segmentation: Recognize the importance of segmenting your target audience based on various demographics, psychographics, and behavioral traits. Explore different segmentation strategies and how they can help you tailor your marketing efforts to specific consumer

groups. By effectively targeting your ideal customers, you can allocate resources efficiently and maximize the effectiveness of your marketing campaigns.

5. Customer Experience: Emphasize the significance of providing exceptional customer experiences. Learn how positive interactions at every touchpoint can influence consumer satisfaction, loyalty, and repeat business. Explore strategies for delivering personalized experiences, addressing customer pain points, and exceeding expectations. By prioritizing customer experience, you can cultivate long-lasting relationships with your customers and build a strong brand reputation.

Understanding the consumer mindset is an ongoing process that requires continuous research, analysis, and adaptation. By staying attuned to evolving consumer preferences and behaviors, you can make informed business decisions and maintain a competitive edge in the marketplace. Through a deep understanding of your target audience, you can create products, services, and marketing campaigns that resonate with consumers, drive profitability, and foster long-term success.

Chapter 5.2: Creating Powerful Marketing Campaigns

Introduction:

In today's highly competitive business landscape, effective marketing is crucial for driving growth, attracting customers, and increasing profitability. In this section, we will explore the art of creating powerful marketing campaigns that capture attention, resonate with your target audience, and drive desired actions. By understanding the key elements of a successful marketing campaign and leveraging proven strategies, you can maximize the impact of your marketing efforts and generate tangible results.

1. Defining Your Campaign Objectives:
    1.1 Setting Clear and Measurable Goals: Determine specific objectives for your marketing campaign, such as increasing brand awareness, driving website traffic, generating leads, or boosting sales.
    1.2 Identifying Target Audience: Clearly define your target audience to tailor your campaign messaging and delivery channels effectively.
    1.3 Understanding Customer Needs and Motivations: Conduct thorough market research and customer analysis to identify the pain points, desires, and motivations of your target audience.

2. Crafting Compelling Campaign Messages:
    2.1 Developing a Unique Selling Proposition (USP): Differentiate your product or service by identifying a compelling USP that highlights its distinct advantages and value to customers.

2.2 Creating Emotional Connections: Tap into the power of emotions by crafting messages that evoke strong feelings and resonate with your target audience on a deeper level.

2.3 Communicating Clear and Concise Messages: Use concise and impactful language to convey your key messages, ensuring they are easily understood and remembered by your audience.

3. Selecting Effective Marketing Channels:

3.1 Leveraging Traditional Channels: Explore traditional marketing channels such as print media, television, radio, and direct mail, considering their relevance to your target audience.

3.2 Harnessing the Power of Digital Channels: Utilize digital marketing channels, including social media platforms, search engine marketing, email marketing, content marketing, and influencer collaborations, to reach a wider audience and engage with potential customers.

3.3 Integrating Multiple Channels: Develop an integrated marketing approach by combining various channels to create a cohesive and consistent brand experience across different touchpoints.

4. Creating Engaging Content:

4.1 Tailoring Content to Different Channels: Customize your content to fit the characteristics and requirements of each marketing channel, ensuring it aligns with the platform and resonates with the intended audience.

4.2 Incorporating Visual and Interactive Elements: Capture attention and increase engagement by using visually appealing graphics, videos, infographics, and interactive elements in your campaign content.

4.3 Implementing Storytelling Techniques: Tell compelling stories that connect with your audience on an emotional level, making your brand memorable and forging deeper connections.

5. Monitoring, Measuring, and Optimizing:

5.1 Tracking Campaign Performance: Establish key performance indicators (KPIs) and use analytics tools to monitor the effectiveness of your marketing campaign, tracking metrics such as impressions, click-through rates, conversions, and return on investment (ROI).

5.2 A/B Testing and Optimization: Continuously test different campaign elements, including headlines, visuals, calls to action, and delivery channels, to optimize performance and improve results.

5.3 Analyzing Data and Making Informed Decisions: Analyze the data collected from your campaign to gain insights, make data-driven decisions, and refine your marketing strategies for future campaigns.

Conclusion:

Creating powerful marketing campaigns requires a combination of strategic planning, creative messaging, and effective execution. By defining clear objectives, understanding your target audience, crafting compelling messages, selecting the right marketing channels, creating engaging content, and continuously monitoring and optimizing your campaigns, you can maximize the impact of your marketing efforts and drive tangible results for your business. Remember,

Chapter 5.3: Building and Managing Sales Channels

In Chapter 5.3 of "Profit Power: Understanding the Art of Making Money," we will explore the critical aspects of building and managing sales channels. Effective sales channels are the lifelines of any business, as they serve as the conduits through which your products or services reach your target customers. By understanding how to build and manage these channels strategically, you can maximize your sales potential and drive sustainable profitability.

1. Understanding Sales Channels:
   1.1 Defining sales channels and their importance in reaching customers
   1.2 Exploring different types of sales channels (e.g., direct sales, retail, online, distribution)
   1.3 Analyzing the pros and cons of various sales channel options

2. Identifying Target Customers:
   2.1 Conducting market research to identify your target customer segments
   2.2 Understanding customer preferences, behaviors, and buying habits
   2.3 Creating customer personas to guide your sales channel decisions

3. Selecting the Right Sales Channels:
   3.1 Evaluating the suitability of different sales channels for your business
   3.2 Assessing the cost-effectiveness and scalability of each channel
   3.3 Developing a multi-channel sales strategy for maximum reach and impact

4. Building and Managing Direct Sales Channels:
   4.1 Establishing a direct sales team or individual sales representatives
   4.2 Developing effective sales training programs
   4.3 Implementing sales performance tracking and measurement systems

5. Leveraging Retail and Online Sales Channels:
   5.1 Understanding the benefits and challenges of retail and online sales
   5.2 Choosing the right retail partners or online platforms
   5.3 Optimizing product placement, pricing, and promotions in retail and online environments

6. Exploring Distribution and Reseller Channels:
   6.1 Identifying potential distribution partners or resellers
   6.2 Negotiating favorable distribution agreements
   6.3 Providing adequate support and incentives for distribution partners

7. Monitoring and Evaluating Sales Channel Performance:
   7.1 Establishing key performance indicators (KPIs) for sales channels
   7.2 Implementing sales analytics and reporting systems
   7.3 Continuously monitoring and optimizing sales channel performance

By diving into Chapter 5.3, you will gain the knowledge and insights needed to build a robust and effective sales channel strategy. Whether you opt for direct sales, retail, online platforms, distribution partnerships, or a combination of these, understanding the intricacies of sales channels will enable you to connect with your target customers, drive sales growth, and ultimately maximize your profit power.

Chapter 6: Managing Finances for Profitability

In the pursuit of building wealth and achieving financial success, it is essential to develop the skills and knowledge required to effectively manage finances. Chapter 6 delves into the crucial topic of managing finances for profitability, recognizing that financial management lies at the heart of any prosperous venture. Whether you are an aspiring entrepreneur, a seasoned business owner, or an individual seeking to optimize your personal finances, understanding the principles and strategies outlined in this chapter will empower you to make sound financial decisions and maximize your profitability.

Managing finances goes beyond simple budgeting; it involves a comprehensive approach to financial planning, analysis, and optimization. In this chapter, we will explore various key aspects of financial management, such as budgeting, cash flow management, financial forecasting, and risk assessment. By mastering these concepts, you will gain the necessary tools to navigate the complex financial landscape and make informed choices that drive profitability.

One of the fundamental pillars of financial management is budgeting. Establishing a well-defined budget allows you to allocate resources efficiently, prioritize spending, and ensure that you have a clear understanding of your financial obligations. We will discuss proven techniques for creating a realistic budget that aligns with your goals and enables you to achieve long-term profitability.

Furthermore, effective cash flow management is crucial for sustaining and growing a profitable enterprise. Understanding cash inflows and outflows, implementing effective collection strategies, and optimizing payment processes are all essential components of managing cash flow. By implementing strategies outlined in this chapter, you will be able to maintain a healthy cash flow and avoid liquidity issues that can hinder your profitability.

Financial forecasting and risk assessment are also integral to successful financial management. By analyzing market trends, identifying potential risks, and projecting future financial performance, you can make proactive decisions to mitigate risks and seize opportunities. We will explore techniques for financial forecasting, risk assessment, and contingency planning, providing you with the tools to navigate uncertainties and maintain profitability in a dynamic business environment.

In conclusion, managing finances for profitability is an indispensable skillset for anyone seeking financial success. By gaining a deep understanding of budgeting, cash flow management, financial forecasting, and risk assessment, you will be well-equipped to make informed financial decisions that enhance profitability and drive long-term success. In the following chapters, we will continue to build upon these principles, exploring further strategies for wealth creation and the achievement of your financial goals.

6.1 Budgeting and Financial Planning

In the realm of profit power, budgeting and financial planning are critical components for achieving long-term financial success. A well-crafted budget serves as a roadmap that guides your financial decisions, allowing you to allocate resources effectively and optimize your profitability. This section will explore the importance of budgeting and provide practical strategies for developing a comprehensive financial plan.

Budgeting involves creating a detailed plan for your income and expenses, ensuring that your financial resources are allocated efficiently. By establishing clear financial goals and tracking your income and expenditures, you gain a deep understanding of your financial position and make informed decisions to maximize your profit potential.

In this section, we will delve into the key steps involved in budgeting and financial planning:

1. Setting Financial Goals: Start by defining your financial objectives, whether it's increasing your savings, reducing debt, or expanding your business. Establishing clear goals provides a sense of purpose and direction for your financial planning process.

2. Tracking Income and Expenses: To create an accurate budget, it's essential to track your income sources and categorize your expenses. Utilize financial software, spreadsheets, or budgeting apps to monitor your cash flow and identify areas where you can optimize your spending.

3. Analyzing Spending Patterns: Review your expenses and identify areas where you can cut costs or reallocate resources. Look for patterns and trends that reveal opportunities for savings or investments that align with your financial goals.

4. Prioritizing and Allocating Resources: Once you have a clear understanding of your income and expenses, prioritize your financial obligations and allocate resources accordingly. Ensure that essential expenses are covered first, such as bills, loan payments, and taxes, and then allocate funds for savings, investments, and discretionary spending.

5. Creating a Contingency Fund: Financial planning is not just about allocating funds; it's also about

preparing for unexpected expenses or emergencies. Set aside a portion of your income for a contingency fund, which acts as a safety net and provides peace of mind in times of financial uncertainty.

6. Reviewing and Adjusting: Regularly review your budget and assess its effectiveness in helping you achieve your financial goals. Adjust your budget as needed, considering changes in income, expenses, or financial circumstances. Flexibility and adaptability are key to maintaining a sustainable financial plan.

By incorporating budgeting and financial planning into your profit power toolkit, you gain greater control over your financial resources, minimize wasteful spending, and optimize your profitability. With a well-structured financial plan, you can make informed decisions, seize opportunities, and navigate economic fluctuations with confidence.

Remember, budgeting is not about restricting yourself; it's about aligning your financial choices with your long-term objectives. Embrace the discipline of budgeting and financial planning, and witness the transformative impact it can have on your path to financial success.

Chapter 6: Managing Finances for Profitability

6.2 Cash Flow Management

In the world of business and finance, cash flow is the lifeblood that sustains and fuels your operations. Effective cash flow management is a critical skill for ensuring the profitability and longevity of your ventures. It involves understanding and optimizing the movement of money into and out of your business to maintain a healthy financial position.

This section will explore key principles and strategies for managing cash flow effectively. By mastering these techniques, you will be able to anticipate and address potential cash flow challenges, seize opportunities for growth, and make informed decisions to maximize profitability.

1. Understanding Cash Flow: Start by gaining a comprehensive understanding of your cash flow patterns. Differentiate between cash inflows (such as sales revenue, loans, or investments) and cash outflows (such as operating expenses, loan repayments, or inventory purchases). By tracking and analyzing these inflows and outflows, you can identify trends, seasonal variations, and potential bottlenecks.

2. Cash Flow Forecasting: Develop a cash flow forecast to project your future cash inflows and outflows. This forward-looking analysis helps you anticipate periods of surplus or shortfall, enabling you to plan accordingly. By understanding your

cash flow needs in advance, you can take proactive measures to bridge any gaps, such as securing additional financing or adjusting spending patterns.

3. Managing Receivables and Payables: Promptly collecting payments from customers and extending payment terms with suppliers are crucial strategies for optimizing cash flow. Implement efficient invoicing and collection processes to minimize delays in receiving payments. Similarly, negotiate favorable payment terms with suppliers to align cash outflows with cash inflows. By balancing the timing of cash inflows and outflows, you can maintain a healthy cash flow position.

4. Controlling Expenses: Evaluate your operating expenses and identify areas where you can reduce costs without compromising the quality of your products or services. Implement cost-saving measures, negotiate favorable contracts with vendors, and regularly review your expense structure to ensure efficiency. By effectively managing expenses, you free up cash that can be reinvested into your business or used to address other financial obligations.

5. Cash Flow Cushion: Building a cash flow cushion or maintaining sufficient cash reserves is essential to navigate unforeseen circumstances or market fluctuations. Unforeseen events such as economic downturns, supply chain disruptions, or unexpected expenses can impact your cash flow. By setting

aside funds for emergencies, you can safeguard your business from potential financial crises and maintain stability.

6. Financing Options: Explore different financing options to support your cash flow needs. From traditional bank loans to lines of credit, invoice factoring, or crowdfunding, there are various avenues to access additional capital when required. Evaluate the terms, costs, and implications of each financing option to determine the most suitable fit for your business.

Remember, cash flow management is an ongoing process that requires regular monitoring and adjustment. Continuously assess your cash flow position, update your forecasts, and adapt your strategies based on changing market conditions or business needs.

By mastering the art of cash flow management, you gain greater control over your financial destiny. A well-managed cash flow ensures that you have the necessary resources to seize opportunities, weather challenges, and ultimately drive profitability and success.

Chapter 6: Managing Finances for Profitability

6.3 Controlling Costs and Maximizing Margins

In the pursuit of profitability, controlling costs and maximizing margins are critical factors that can significantly impact the financial health of your business. By effectively managing expenses and optimizing your pricing strategy, you can enhance your bottom line and strengthen your competitive position in the market.

In this section, we will explore strategies and best practices for cost control and margin optimization, helping you make informed decisions and achieve sustainable profitability.

1. Cost Analysis and Reduction:
   - Conduct a comprehensive analysis of your business's expenses, categorizing them into fixed and variable costs.
   - Identify areas where cost reductions can be made without compromising the quality of your products or services.
   - Seek opportunities to negotiate better deals with suppliers, explore bulk purchasing options, or consider alternative vendors.
   - Implement cost-saving measures such as energy efficiency initiatives, waste reduction programs, and process optimization.

2. Efficient Inventory Management:
   - Implement inventory management systems to ensure optimal stock levels, minimizing the risk of overstocking or stockouts.

- Use forecasting techniques and historical data to estimate demand accurately and plan inventory accordingly.
- Regularly review and update your inventory to identify slow-moving or obsolete items and take necessary actions to liquidate or discontinue them.

3. Streamlined Operations:
- Continuously assess your business processes and workflows to identify bottlenecks or inefficiencies.
- Implement automation or technology solutions where appropriate to streamline operations and reduce manual errors.
- Foster a culture of continuous improvement, encouraging employees to suggest ideas for enhancing operational efficiency.

4. Pricing Strategy:
- Conduct market research and competitor analysis to gain insights into pricing trends and customer expectations.
- Determine your product's value proposition and position it accordingly in the market.
- Consider dynamic pricing strategies, such as tiered pricing or promotional offers, to maximize revenue based on demand fluctuations.
- Regularly review and adjust your pricing strategy based on market conditions, cost changes, and customer feedback.

5. Value-Added Services:

- Identify opportunities to offer additional services or complementary products that can increase the overall value for your customers.
- Assess the feasibility of upselling or cross-selling to existing customers to enhance their experience and increase average transaction value.
- Focus on building strong customer relationships and providing exceptional service to encourage customer loyalty and repeat business.

6. Continuous Financial Monitoring:
- Implement robust financial tracking and reporting systems to monitor key financial metrics and identify areas of concern.
- Regularly review your financial statements, including profit and loss statements, cash flow statements, and balance sheets.
- Conduct variance analysis to compare actual performance against budgeted targets and identify deviations for further investigation.
- Engage with financial professionals or consultants to gain valuable insights and advice on optimizing your financial management practices.

By implementing these strategies and approaches, you can take control of your costs, improve your profit margins, and enhance the overall financial performance of your business. Remember, cost control and margin optimization are ongoing efforts that require vigilance, adaptability, and a commitment to continuous improvement. Stay focused, make data-driven decisions, and strive for excellence in managing your finances for profitability.

Chapter 7: Investing for Long-Term Profit

In Chapter 7 of our book, "The Mindset of Wealth," we delve into the captivating realm of investing for long-term profit. Building upon the principles and knowledge shared in previous chapters, this chapter aims to equip you with the understanding and strategies necessary to navigate the complex world of investments.

Investing has long been regarded as a powerful tool for creating wealth and securing a prosperous future. However, it is important to approach investing with a discerning mindset and a comprehensive understanding of the various investment options available. The key lies in making informed decisions, based on a sound financial foundation and a clear long-term vision.

Throughout this chapter, we will explore the principles and strategies that successful investors employ to achieve sustainable financial growth. We will delve into the intricacies of different investment vehicles, such as stocks, bonds, real estate, and mutual funds, shedding light on their potential risks and rewards.

Understanding the importance of diversification and risk management will be central to our discussion.

We will emphasize the significance of a well-balanced portfolio, which includes a mix of high-growth investments and more stable, income-generating assets. By learning how to allocate your resources wisely and adapt to changing market conditions, you can enhance your chances of long-term profitability.

Moreover, we will explore the role of patience and discipline in investing. Successful investors understand that wealth creation is a gradual process, and they refrain from succumbing to impulsive decisions driven by short-term market fluctuations. We will discuss the value of setting realistic financial goals and developing a disciplined investment strategy that aligns with your risk tolerance and time horizon.

In addition to traditional investment methods, we will also explore the potential of emerging technologies and alternative investment avenues. The rapid advancement of financial technology has opened up new possibilities for investors, enabling them to access global markets, engage in peer-to-peer lending, and explore the exciting world of cryptocurrencies and blockchain technology.

As we navigate the intricate landscape of investing for long-term profit, it is crucial to remember that knowledge and continuous learning are the keys to success. This chapter aims to provide you with a solid foundation and the essential tools to make informed investment decisions that align with your financial goals.

By mastering the principles outlined in this chapter, you will be empowered to navigate the dynamic nature of financial markets, seize opportunities, and ultimately build wealth for yourself and future generations. So, let us embark on this enlightening journey and unlock the secrets of investing for long-term profit.

Chapter 7.1: Understanding Economic Cycles

Introduction:

In the world of finance and business, economic cycles play a crucial role in shaping the opportunities and challenges that individuals and organizations encounter. Understanding these cycles is essential for navigating the ever-changing economic landscape and making informed decisions to maximize profitability. In this section, we will explore the concept of economic cycles, their phases, and the key factors that drive them.

1. The Nature of Economic Cycles:

1.1 Definition and Overview:
 - What are economic cycles?
 - The relationship between economic growth and contraction.
 - Historical examples of economic cycles.

1.2 Duration and Patterns:
   - The typical length of economic cycles.
   - Recurring patterns and characteristics.
   - The role of technological advancements in shaping cycles.

2. Phases of Economic Cycles:

2.1 Expansion Phase:
   - Characteristics of the expansion phase.
   - Factors driving economic growth.
   - Opportunities and strategies for profit during expansion.

2.2 Peak Phase:
   - Identifying signs of a peak in the economic cycle.
   - Potential risks and challenges during the peak phase.
   - Strategies for managing risks and maintaining profitability.

2.3 Contraction Phase:
   - Understanding economic downturns and recessions.
   - Impact on businesses and individuals.
   - Navigating challenges and preserving financial stability.

2.4 Trough Phase:
   - Characteristics of the trough phase.

- Indicators of recovery and the beginning of a new cycle.
- Positioning for future growth and profitability.

3. Key Factors Influencing Economic Cycles:

3.1 Monetary Policy:
- The role of central banks in managing economic cycles.
- Interest rates, inflation, and their impact on business activities.
- Strategies for adapting to changing monetary policies.

3.2 Fiscal Policy:
- Government spending and taxation policies.
- Stimulus measures and their effects on the economy.
- Anticipating and leveraging fiscal policies for profit.

3.3 Global Factors:
- International trade and globalization's influence on economic cycles.
- Geopolitical events and their impact on global economies.
- Identifying global trends and adapting to global economic shifts.

4. Tools for Navigating Economic Cycles:

4.1 Economic Indicators:

- Key indicators to monitor economic health.
- Using leading and lagging indicators to forecast trends.
- Incorporating economic data into decision-making processes.

4.2 Risk Management Strategies:
- Mitigating risks during economic downturns.
- Diversification and portfolio management techniques.
- Capitalizing on opportunities during economic upswings.

4.3 Long-Term Planning:
- Creating resilient business strategies.
- Aligning long-term goals with economic cycles.
- Building financial buffers and contingency plans.

Conclusion:

Understanding economic cycles is an invaluable skill for individuals and businesses seeking sustained profitability. By recognizing the different phases of economic cycles, adapting to changing conditions, and leveraging key factors influencing these cycles, you can position yourself for success in any economic climate. In the next sections, we will explore how to identify and capitalize on market trends, and strategies for thriving in challenging times. Stay tuned for insights on how to harness the profit power within economic cycles.

Chapter 7: Investing for Long-Term Profit

Section 7.2: Developing an Investment Strategy

Investing is a powerful tool for wealth creation and long-term profit. However, successful investing requires careful planning, research, and the development of a well-defined investment strategy. In this section, we will delve into the key considerations and steps involved in crafting an effective investment strategy that aligns with your financial goals and risk tolerance.

1. Defining Your Investment Goals: Begin by clearly defining your investment objectives. Are you aiming for capital appreciation, generating passive income, or preserving wealth? Understanding your goals will help shape the investment strategy that best suits your needs.

2. Assessing Your Risk Tolerance: Every investor has a unique risk tolerance, which determines their comfort level with potential losses. Assess your risk tolerance by considering factors such as your financial situation, time horizon, and emotional ability to withstand market fluctuations. This assessment will guide you in selecting investments that align with your risk profile.

3. Asset Allocation: Asset allocation refers to the distribution of your investment portfolio across different asset classes, such as stocks, bonds, real

estate, and commodities. A well-diversified portfolio can help manage risk and optimize returns. Determine the appropriate allocation based on your risk tolerance, investment goals, and market conditions.

4. Research and Due Diligence: Thorough research is essential before making any investment decisions. Study the underlying fundamentals of the assets you are considering, analyze market trends, and evaluate the potential risks and rewards. Consider seeking professional advice or using investment tools to aid your research process.

5. Investment Vehicles: There are various investment vehicles available, including stocks, bonds, mutual funds, exchange-traded funds (ETFs), real estate, and more. Understand the characteristics, risks, and potential returns associated with each investment option. Choose vehicles that align with your investment strategy and diversification goals.

6. Time Horizon: Consider your investment time horizon, which refers to the length of time you plan to hold your investments. Different assets may perform differently over various time frames. Align your investments with your time horizon to maximize the potential for long-term profit.

7. Regular Monitoring and Rebalancing: Once you have built your investment portfolio, regularly

monitor its performance and make necessary adjustments. Market conditions, asset performance, and changes in your financial situation may require rebalancing your portfolio to maintain the desired asset allocation and risk exposure.

8. Risk Management: Mitigating risk is a crucial aspect of successful investing. Implement risk management strategies such as setting stop-loss orders, diversifying across assets and sectors, and having a contingency plan for unexpected events. Remember, no investment is entirely risk-free, but proper risk management can help protect your capital.

9. Reviewing and Adjusting: Regularly review your investment strategy to ensure it remains aligned with your goals, risk tolerance, and changing market conditions. Adjustments may be necessary as your financial situation evolves or when new opportunities arise.

Developing an investment strategy requires thoughtful consideration, analysis, and adaptability. It is essential to stay informed, be disciplined, and avoid emotional decision-making. By following these steps and refining your strategy over time, you can increase your chances of achieving long-term profit and financial success.

Remember, investing involves uncertainty, and past performance is not indicative of future results. It is advisable to seek professional advice and continually educate yourself about investment principles and market dynamics to make informed decisions.

Chapter 7: Investing for Long-Term Profit

Section 7.3: Diversification and Risk Management

In the pursuit of long-term profitability, one of the most crucial aspects of investing is diversification and risk management. While investing inherently involves taking on a certain degree of risk, a well-diversified portfolio can help mitigate potential losses and maximize returns. In this section, we will explore the importance of diversification and provide insights into effective risk management strategies.

7.3.1 Understanding Diversification

Diversification is the practice of spreading your investments across different asset classes, industries, geographic regions, and investment types. By doing so, you can reduce the overall risk of your portfolio. The principle behind diversification is that different investments react differently to market conditions. When one investment is experiencing a decline, another may be performing well, balancing out the overall performance of your portfolio.

7.3.2 Building a Diversified Portfolio

To build a diversified portfolio, you should consider investing in a mix of assets such as stocks, bonds, real estate, commodities, and alternative investments. Additionally, spreading your investments across different sectors and industries can further enhance diversification. The goal is to create a portfolio that is not overly concentrated in a single investment or asset class, as this can expose you to unnecessary risk.

7.3.3 Risk Management Strategies

While diversification is a key component of risk management, it is important to supplement it with other risk management strategies. Some common risk management techniques include:

a) Asset Allocation: Allocating your investments across different asset classes based on your risk tolerance, investment goals, and time horizon. This helps balance risk and return potential.

b) Regular Portfolio Rebalancing: Periodically reviewing and adjusting your portfolio to maintain the desired asset allocation. Rebalancing ensures that your portfolio remains aligned with your investment objectives and helps control risk.

c) Stop-Loss Orders: Placing stop-loss orders on individual investments to limit potential losses. A stop-loss order automatically sells a security if it reaches a predetermined price, protecting your investment from significant declines.

d) Hedging Strategies: Employing hedging techniques, such as using options or futures contracts, to offset potential losses in one investment with gains in another. Hedging can help protect your portfolio against adverse market movements.

e) Risk Assessment and Monitoring: Continuously evaluating and monitoring the risk associated with your investments. This includes staying informed about market trends, analyzing company fundamentals, and keeping track of economic indicators that may impact your portfolio.

Remember, risk management is an ongoing process that requires regular assessment and adjustment. It is essential to review your portfolio periodically, reassess your risk tolerance, and make necessary modifications to align with changing market conditions and personal circumstances.

By effectively diversifying your investments and implementing sound risk management strategies, you can position yourself for long-term profit while mitigating potential losses. Achieving a balance between risk and return is key to successful investing. So, take the time to carefully consider your investment decisions, seek professional advice when needed, and stay disciplined in your approach to maximize your profit potential while managing risk.

Note: The strategies and concepts discussed in this section are meant for informational purposes only and should not be considered as financial advice. Consult with a qualified financial advisor or investment professional before making any investment decisions.

Chapter 8: Leveraging Technology for Profit

Introduction:

In today's rapidly evolving digital age, technology has become an integral part of our lives, transforming the way we work, communicate, and conduct business. The constant advancements in technology have created unprecedented opportunities for individuals and businesses to leverage its power and unlock new pathways to profitability. Chapter 8 of our book delves into the exciting realm of leveraging technology for profit, equipping you with the knowledge and strategies to harness the full potential of technological innovations.

From artificial intelligence and machine learning to blockchain and automation, technology has revolutionized industries across the globe, disrupting traditional business models and creating new avenues for growth. This chapter explores how you can embrace these technological advancements to optimize your operations, enhance customer experiences, and drive your profitability to new heights.

We will begin by discussing the importance of staying abreast of emerging technologies and trends, as well as the mindset required to effectively integrate technology into your business. With a solid understanding of the transformative power of technology, we will then explore specific strategies and tools that can be utilized to leverage its potential.

Effective utilization of technology can streamline processes, boost productivity, and enable you to reach a wider audience. We will delve into the world of digital marketing, exploring the myriad of online platforms and strategies available to expand your reach and connect with customers in a targeted and cost-effective manner. We will also discuss the importance of data analytics and how it can empower you to make informed business decisions, optimize your marketing campaigns, and personalize your offerings to meet customer needs.

Moreover, we will explore the realm of financial technology (FinTech) and its impact on various sectors, such as banking, investments, and payment systems. We will examine how FinTech solutions can enhance financial management, provide access to alternative funding sources, and streamline transaction processes, ultimately contributing to your bottom line.

Additionally, this chapter will touch upon the potential risks and challenges associated with technology implementation, such as cybersecurity threats and the need for ongoing training and adaptation. By understanding these challenges, you can proactively mitigate risks and ensure the long-term sustainability of your technological investments.

As you progress through this chapter, you will gain valuable insights and practical guidance on how to effectively leverage technology for profit. Whether you are a small business owner, an aspiring entrepreneur, or a seasoned professional, the principles and strategies outlined in this chapter will empower you to navigate the digital landscape with confidence and seize the myriad opportunities it presents.

Prepare to embark on a transformative journey as we explore the vast potential of technology and its profound impact on profitability. By embracing technology and adapting to the digital era, you can position yourself and your business at the forefront of innovation, setting the stage for sustainable growth and success in the dynamic and ever-evolving business landscape.

Chapter 8.1: Embracing the Digital Revolution

In today's fast-paced and interconnected world, technology has become an integral part of our lives. The digital revolution has transformed industries, disrupted traditional business models, and created unprecedented opportunities for profit and growth.

In this chapter, we will explore the importance of embracing the digital revolution and how it can enhance your profitability.

1. The Power of Digital Transformation
    1.1 Understanding Digital Transformation
    1.2 The Benefits of Digital Transformation
    1.3 Case Studies: Successful Digital Transformation Stories

2. Harnessing Technology for Operational Efficiency
    2.1 Automation and Streamlining Processes
    2.2 Cloud Computing and Scalability
    2.3 Optimizing Supply Chain with Technology

3. Enhancing Customer Experience through Digital Channels
    3.1 Leveraging Social Media and Online Presence
    3.2 Personalization and Customer Relationship Management
    3.3 E-commerce and Online Sales Strategies

4. Data Analytics and Business Intelligence
    4.1 Leveraging Data for Decision-Making
    4.2 Implementing Effective Data Analytics Tools
    4.3 Predictive Analytics and Business Insights

5. Cybersecurity and Risk Management
    5.1 Understanding Cyber Threats and Risks
    5.2 Implementing Robust Security Measures

5.3 Creating a Culture of Cybersecurity

6. Embracing Emerging Technologies
   6.1 Artificial Intelligence and Machine Learning
   6.2 Internet of Things (IoT) and Connectivity
   6.3 Blockchain and Distributed Ledger Technology

7. Adaptability and Agility in the Digital Age
   7.1 Embracing a Growth Mindset
   7.2 Continuous Learning and Upskilling
   7.3 Staying Ahead of Technological Advancements

8. Ethical Considerations in the Digital World
   8.1 Privacy and Data Protection
   8.2 Responsible Use of Artificial Intelligence
   8.3 Ensuring Equity and Inclusion in Digital Transformation

By embracing the digital revolution, you can unlock new avenues of profit, enhance operational efficiency, improve customer experiences, and gain valuable insights for strategic decision-making. However, it is essential to navigate the digital landscape responsibly, considering ethical considerations and managing potential risks. In this chapter, we will provide you with the knowledge and tools to navigate this exciting digital era and harness its full potential for profitability and success.

Chapter 8.2: Using Technology to Streamline Operations

In today's rapidly advancing digital landscape, technology has become a driving force behind business success. By leveraging technological tools and innovations, entrepreneurs and organizations can streamline their operations, boost efficiency, and gain a competitive edge. In this chapter, we will explore various ways to utilize technology effectively and optimize your business processes for maximum profitability.

1. Automating Routine Tasks: Technology offers a plethora of automation solutions that can save time and resources. By automating repetitive and mundane tasks such as data entry, inventory management, and invoicing, you can free up valuable human capital to focus on more strategic activities that contribute directly to profit generation.

2. Implementing Cloud Computing: Cloud computing provides a flexible and scalable infrastructure for businesses of all sizes. It enables you to store and access data, applications, and software on remote servers, eliminating the need for costly on-premises hardware. Cloud computing offers advantages such as enhanced collaboration, increased data security, and reduced IT maintenance costs.

3. Adopting Customer Relationship Management (CRM) Systems: A CRM system allows you to effectively manage and nurture customer relationships. It provides a centralized database for storing customer information, interactions, and preferences, enabling personalized marketing and sales efforts. With a CRM system in place, you can streamline customer communication, improve lead generation, and enhance customer satisfaction and retention.

4. Utilizing Project Management Tools: Project management tools facilitate efficient planning, organization, and execution of tasks and projects. These tools enable collaboration, task assignment, progress tracking, and deadline management. By adopting project management software, you can ensure timely completion of projects, minimize bottlenecks, and optimize resource allocation, leading to increased profitability.

5. Implementing Data Analytics and Business Intelligence: The vast amount of data available today holds valuable insights that can drive profit growth. Data analytics and business intelligence tools help extract meaningful patterns, trends, and correlations from data, enabling informed decision-making. By leveraging data analytics, you can identify customer preferences, optimize pricing strategies, detect market trends, and uncover areas for cost savings and process improvement.

6. Enhancing Communication and Collaboration: Technology facilitates seamless communication and collaboration within your organization and with external stakeholders. Utilize tools such as video conferencing, instant messaging, and project collaboration platforms to enhance team productivity, foster innovation, and strengthen relationships with customers, suppliers, and partners.

7. Embracing E-commerce and Online Marketing: The internet and e-commerce have revolutionized the way businesses operate and reach customers. Establishing an online presence through e-commerce platforms and implementing online marketing strategies allows you to expand your customer base, increase sales, and reduce overhead costs associated with physical storefronts. Leverage digital marketing techniques such as search engine optimization (SEO), social media marketing, and targeted advertising to drive traffic, engage customers, and maximize conversion rates.

8. Ensuring Cybersecurity and Data Protection: As technology advances, the need for robust cybersecurity measures becomes paramount. Protecting sensitive customer data, financial information, and intellectual property is crucial for maintaining trust and preventing costly breaches. Implement security protocols, encryption methods,

and regular data backups to safeguard your business and mitigate cyber threats.

By incorporating these technological advancements into your business operations, you can optimize efficiency, reduce costs, and drive profitability. However, it is important to carefully assess your specific needs, consider scalability, and invest in proper training and support to maximize the benefits of technology. Embrace the power of technology to streamline your operations, unlock new opportunities, and stay ahead in today's fast-paced business landscape.

Chapter 8: Leveraging Technology for Profit

8.3 Harnessing the Power of Data and Analytics

In today's digital age, data has become a valuable asset for businesses seeking to maximize their profitability. The ability to collect, analyze, and leverage data can provide invaluable insights and drive informed decision-making. In this section, we will explore the power of data and analytics and how you can harness them to enhance your profitability.

1. The Importance of Data-Driven Decision Making:
　1.1 Understanding the value of data in business
　1.2 Making decisions based on data and evidence

1.3 Overcoming challenges in data-driven decision making

2. Collecting and Managing Data Effectively:
    2.1 Identifying relevant data sources
    2.2 Implementing robust data collection processes
    2.3 Ensuring data accuracy, reliability, and security

3. Analyzing and Interpreting Data:
    3.1 Exploring different data analysis techniques
    3.2 Using data visualization tools for better insights
    3.3 Identifying patterns, trends, and correlations in data

4. Leveraging Predictive Analytics:
    4.1 Understanding the concept of predictive analytics
    4.2 Applying predictive modeling techniques
    4.3 Anticipating customer behavior and market trends

5. Personalization and Targeted Marketing:
    5.1 Using data to create personalized customer experiences
    5.2 Implementing targeted marketing campaigns
    5.3 Maximizing customer engagement and conversion rates

6. Operational Efficiency and Process Optimization:

6.1 Applying data analytics to improve operational efficiency
6.2 Optimizing supply chain and inventory management
6.3 Reducing costs and enhancing productivity through data insights

7. Mitigating Risks and Enhancing Security:
7.1 Identifying potential risks through data analysis
7.2 Implementing data-driven risk management strategies
7.3 Enhancing data security and protecting sensitive information

8. Embracing Artificial Intelligence and Machine Learning:
8.1 Understanding the role of AI and ML in data analysis
8.2 Leveraging AI-powered tools and algorithms
8.3 Automating processes and gaining predictive insights

By harnessing the power of data and analytics, you can gain a competitive edge, optimize your operations, and make informed decisions that drive profitability. Whether you are a small business owner, an entrepreneur, or a corporate executive, understanding how to effectively collect, analyze, and leverage data will position you for success in the digital era.

Remember, data is not just numbers; it represents valuable insights into your customers, market trends, and operational efficiency. Embrace the potential of data and analytics, and unlock new avenues for growth and profitability in your business.

Chapter 9: Navigating Economic Cycles and Trends

In the ever-changing landscape of the global economy, understanding how to navigate economic cycles and trends is crucial for anyone seeking to build and sustain wealth. The world of finance and markets can be volatile and unpredictable, influenced by a multitude of factors such as technological advancements, geopolitical events, and shifting consumer behaviors. Successfully navigating these ebbs and flows requires a combination of knowledge, foresight, and adaptability.

Chapter 9 delves into the intricate world of economic cycles and trends, providing invaluable insights and strategies to help you capitalize on opportunities and mitigate risks. By gaining a deeper understanding of these cycles and trends, you will be better equipped to make informed financial decisions, safeguard your investments, and position yourself for long-term profitability.

Throughout this chapter, we will explore various economic indicators and tools used to analyze and predict market movements. We will discuss the different phases of economic cycles, from periods of expansion and growth to times of contraction and recession. Understanding the characteristics and patterns of each phase will enable you to identify signals and adjust your financial strategies accordingly.

Moreover, we will explore the impact of trends and disruptive forces on the economy and industries. Technological advancements, demographic shifts, and changes in consumer preferences have the potential to reshape entire sectors and create new opportunities for wealth creation. By staying attuned to these trends, you can position yourself at the forefront of innovation and capitalize on emerging markets.

In this chapter, you will also discover strategies to navigate economic downturns and turbulent times. We will explore risk management techniques, portfolio diversification, and the importance of maintaining a long-term perspective in the face of short-term market fluctuations. By adopting a proactive and resilient mindset, you can weather economic storms and emerge stronger on the other side.

Remember, the world of finance is dynamic and ever-evolving. By developing a deep understanding of economic cycles and trends, you can navigate the complexities of the global marketplace with confidence and make informed decisions that pave the way to long-term profitability. So, join us as we embark on a journey through the fascinating realm of economic cycles and trends, and equip yourself with the knowledge and skills to thrive in an ever-changing financial landscape.

9.1 The Importance of Setting Financial Goals

In the journey toward financial success and profitability, setting clear and achievable financial goals is of paramount importance. Without a target to aim for, it becomes challenging to make informed decisions, prioritize your efforts, and measure your progress. In this section, we explore the significance of setting financial goals and how they can propel you toward long-term profitability.

Financial goals provide a sense of direction and purpose. They help you establish a roadmap for your financial journey, allowing you to envision the future you desire and articulate the steps required to get there. Whether your goals involve starting a successful business, achieving a certain level of income, or building a robust investment portfolio, they serve as guiding beacons, keeping you focused and motivated.

Moreover, setting financial goals enables you to prioritize your actions and allocate resources effectively. By defining what matters most to you and aligning your financial decisions with your goals, you can avoid distractions and make choices that propel you forward. It allows you to assess opportunities and determine if they align with your long-term objectives, ensuring that your efforts and resources are channeled toward activities that contribute to your financial success.

Financial goals also serve as benchmarks for measuring progress and celebrating achievements. As you break down your larger objectives into smaller, manageable milestones, you gain a clear sense of progress along the way. This not only boosts your confidence but also allows you to course-correct if necessary, ensuring that you stay on track to achieve your ultimate financial goals.

Additionally, setting financial goals provides a framework for accountability and discipline. By committing to specific targets and timelines, you establish a sense of responsibility to yourself and your financial future. This encourages you to make consistent, proactive choices that align with your goals, such as disciplined saving, prudent spending, and strategic investment decisions.

It's important to note that financial goals should be both challenging and realistic. While it's essential to aim high and push yourself outside of your comfort zone, setting unattainable goals can lead to frustration and demotivation. Take into account your current financial situation, resources, and capabilities when defining your goals. Break them down into smaller, achievable steps that provide a sense of progress and momentum.

Regularly reviewing and reassessing your financial goals is crucial as well. As circumstances change, you may need to modify your goals to reflect new opportunities, challenges, or personal priorities. Flexibility and adaptability are key to maintaining relevance and ensuring that your goals remain aligned with your evolving financial landscape.

In conclusion, setting financial goals is a fundamental step toward achieving profitability and long-term financial success. They provide direction, help prioritize your efforts, measure progress, and foster discipline and accountability. By setting clear, challenging, and realistic goals, you empower yourself to make informed decisions and navigate your financial journey with purpose and intention. Embrace the power of goal-setting and unlock your full potential on the path to profitability.

9.2 Identifying and Capitalizing on Market Trends

In the ever-changing landscape of business and finance, market trends play a crucial role in shaping opportunities for profitability. Being able to identify emerging trends and capitalize on them can give you a competitive edge and propel your financial success. In this section, we will explore strategies to effectively identify and leverage market trends.

1. Market Research: Thorough market research is the foundation for understanding current and future trends. Stay informed about your industry, target

market, and consumer behavior. Utilize market research tools, conduct surveys, and analyze data to gain valuable insights into customer preferences, needs, and emerging patterns.

2. Stay Ahead of the Curve: Successful entrepreneurs and investors are often early adopters of emerging trends. Keep a keen eye on industry developments, technological advancements, and societal shifts. By staying ahead of the curve, you position yourself to seize opportunities before they become mainstream.

3. Network and Collaborate: Engage with industry professionals, thought leaders, and innovators. Attend conferences, join industry associations, and participate in networking events. Collaborating with others can provide fresh perspectives and early access to insider information about upcoming trends.

4. Monitor Consumer Behavior: Consumer behavior is a powerful indicator of market trends. Pay attention to changing consumer preferences, buying patterns, and social influences. Stay attuned to shifts in demographics, lifestyles, and values that may impact market dynamics.

5. Analyze Data: Data analytics can provide valuable insights into market trends. Leverage tools and technologies that allow you to collect and analyze data effectively. Identify patterns,

correlations, and outliers to understand market trends and make informed decisions.

6. Embrace Technology: Technology often drives market trends. Stay updated on advancements in your industry and explore how new technologies can disrupt or create opportunities. Embracing technology can help you adapt to changing market dynamics and position yourself for success.

7. Follow Thought Leaders and Influencers: Identify key thought leaders and influencers in your industry. Follow their publications, blogs, social media channels, and participate in relevant discussions. Thought leaders often provide valuable insights and predictions about future trends.

8. Experiment and Iterate: Stay agile and be willing to experiment with new ideas and strategies. Test different approaches, measure their impact, and iterate based on feedback and results. Flexibility and adaptability are essential when it comes to capitalizing on market trends.

9. Focus on Customer Experience: A deep understanding of customer needs and desires is paramount. By providing an exceptional customer experience, you can build loyalty and gain valuable feedback that helps you identify emerging trends. Listen to your customers, adapt your offerings, and anticipate their future demands.

Remember, identifying and capitalizing on market trends requires a combination of research, intuition, and a willingness to take calculated risks. Stay curious, be proactive, and continuously seek knowledge to position yourself as a trendsetter in your industry. By effectively leveraging market trends, you can stay ahead of the competition and unlock new avenues of profitability.

Chapter 9.3: Strategies for Thriving in Challenging Times

In the ever-changing landscape of the business world, encountering challenging times is inevitable. Economic downturns, market fluctuations, and unexpected disruptions can test even the most resilient entrepreneurs and investors. However, with the right strategies and mindset, it is possible not only to survive but also to thrive during these difficult periods. In this section, we will explore effective strategies for navigating and overcoming challenges, ensuring that your profitability remains intact.

1. Stay Agile and Adapt: In challenging times, the ability to adapt quickly and embrace change is paramount. Assess the situation, identify emerging trends, and make necessary adjustments to your business model or investment strategy. Stay attuned to market shifts and be willing to pivot,

seize new opportunities, or explore alternative revenue streams.

2. Focus on Core Competencies: During challenging times, it's crucial to concentrate your efforts on your core strengths and areas of expertise. Evaluate your business or investment portfolio and determine where your competitive advantage lies. By honing in on what sets you apart, you can allocate resources effectively and maintain a strong position in the market.

3. Cut Costs without Sacrificing Quality: Implementing cost-cutting measures can help weather financial storms. Analyze your expenses and identify areas where you can reduce costs without compromising quality or customer satisfaction. Negotiate better deals with suppliers, streamline operations, and eliminate non-essential expenditures to improve your bottom line.

4. Build Strong Relationships: Strong relationships with customers, partners, and suppliers can be invaluable during challenging times. Nurture these connections by providing exceptional service, maintaining open lines of communication, and demonstrating your commitment to their success. Collaborate with strategic partners to find mutually beneficial solutions and explore new markets or revenue-sharing opportunities.

5. Enhance Customer Value: Focus on delivering exceptional value to your customers, even during challenging periods. Understand their evolving needs and tailor your products or services accordingly. Offer flexible payment options, personalized support, or loyalty incentives to cultivate customer loyalty and maintain a competitive edge.

6. Preserve Cash Flow: Cash flow management is critical during challenging times. Review your cash flow projections regularly, ensure timely collection of receivables, and negotiate extended payment terms with vendors when feasible. Explore additional funding sources or seek assistance from financial institutions to maintain a healthy cash flow position.

7. Seek Professional Advice: Don't hesitate to seek guidance from professionals during challenging times. Engage with experienced advisors, mentors, or industry experts who can provide insights, share best practices, and offer valuable guidance tailored to your specific circumstances. Their expertise can help you navigate through uncertainties and make informed decisions.

8. Monitor and Manage Risks: Identify and assess potential risks that may arise during challenging periods. Develop risk mitigation strategies, such as diversifying your investments, implementing insurance coverage, or creating contingency plans.

Regularly review and update your risk management framework to ensure its relevance and effectiveness.

9. Maintain a Positive Mindset: Lastly, maintaining a positive mindset is crucial when facing challenges. While it is normal to experience setbacks or obstacles, view them as opportunities for growth and learning. Stay focused, remain resilient, and visualize success even in the face of adversity. Surround yourself with a supportive network that can provide encouragement and motivation during challenging times.

By employing these strategies, you can navigate through challenging times with confidence and resilience. Remember, difficult periods often present hidden opportunities for growth and innovation. Embrace the challenge, adapt to the changing landscape, and emerge stronger, ultimately harnessing the profit power within you.

Chapter 10: Building Wealth and Leaving a Legacy

In the pursuit of financial success, it is essential to adopt a long-term perspective that extends beyond one's personal accumulation of wealth. Chapter 10 delves into the vital topic of building wealth and leaving a lasting legacy. This chapter explores the notion that true prosperity lies not only in the accumulation of material riches but also in the impact one leaves on future generations and society as a whole.

Building wealth is a multifaceted endeavor that requires careful planning, disciplined action, and an unwavering commitment to personal growth. However, the path to true prosperity transcends mere financial gains. It entails embracing a broader perspective and understanding the importance of creating a positive and lasting impact that extends far beyond one's own lifetime.

In this final chapter, we will delve into the principles and strategies that can guide individuals toward building a legacy that goes beyond financial success. We will explore the various dimensions of wealth, including intellectual, emotional, and social capital. Moreover, we will examine the importance of giving back, philanthropy, and contributing to the betterment of society.

To build a lasting legacy, it is crucial to consider the values that underpin one's actions and decisions. We will delve into the significance of ethics, integrity, and responsible stewardship in wealth creation. By incorporating these principles into our financial endeavors, we can ensure that our success not only benefits ourselves but also serves as a source of inspiration and upliftment for others.

Furthermore, this chapter will provide insights into the practical aspects of legacy-building, including estate planning, generational wealth transfer, and establishing enduring institutions that can carry forward one's vision and values. We will explore the power of education and mentorship in shaping future generations and equipping them with the knowledge and skills necessary for their own financial independence and success.

Ultimately, building wealth and leaving a legacy is about creating a ripple effect of positive change that extends far beyond our individual lives. By embracing this mindset, we can transform our pursuit of prosperity into a purpose-driven journey that not only enriches our own lives but also uplifts the lives of those around us and leaves a lasting impact on the world. Let us embark on this final chapter with a renewed dedication to building wealth, living purposefully, and leaving a legacy that will endure for generations to come.

10.1 Creating Long-Term Financial Security

In the pursuit of profit, it is essential to look beyond immediate gains and consider the importance of long-term financial security. Building wealth is not just about accumulating money in the present; it is about creating a sustainable and secure financial future.

To establish long-term financial security, it is crucial to focus on several key aspects:

1. Setting Clear Financial Goals: Define your long-term financial objectives, such as retirement planning, education funds for your children, or owning a home. Setting clear goals helps you establish a roadmap for your financial journey.

2. Developing a Comprehensive Financial Plan: Craft a well-rounded financial plan that encompasses savings, investments, insurance, and tax strategies. A holistic approach ensures that you address various aspects of your financial life and optimize your resources.

3. Emphasizing Savings and Budgeting: Cultivate a habit of regular savings by creating a budget that aligns with your financial goals. By tracking and managing your expenses, you can allocate funds towards savings and investments, thereby building a solid financial foundation.

4. Building Emergency Funds: Prepare for unexpected events by establishing an emergency fund. Having a financial safety net enables you to navigate unforeseen circumstances without jeopardizing your long-term financial security.

5. Diversifying Investments: Spread your investments across different asset classes to minimize risk and maximize returns. Diversification helps protect your wealth from market volatility and ensures a more stable financial portfolio.

6. Continuously Educating Yourself: Stay updated on financial trends, investment opportunities, and tax regulations. Financial markets evolve, and staying informed equips you to make informed decisions and adapt to changing circumstances.

7. Regularly Assessing and Adjusting Your Plan: Review and reassess your financial plan periodically to account for changes in your life, such as marriage, children, career transitions, or economic shifts. Adjustments ensure that your plan remains relevant and aligned with your evolving goals.

8. Seeking Professional Advice: Consider consulting with a financial advisor or planner who can provide personalized guidance tailored to your unique circumstances. Professional expertise can offer valuable insights and help you make informed decisions based on your financial aspirations.

9. Mitigating Risks: Understand and mitigate potential risks to your financial security, such as insurance coverage for health, life, and property. Adequate risk management safeguards your wealth and provides peace of mind.

10. Maintaining Discipline and Patience: Building long-term financial security requires discipline and patience. Stay focused on your goals, avoid impulsive decisions, and adhere to your financial plan even during periods of market volatility.

By implementing these strategies and principles, you can create a solid foundation for long-term financial security. Remember, the journey to wealth is not a sprint but a marathon. Stay committed, adapt to changing circumstances, and make prudent financial decisions that align with your aspirations for a secure future.

Chapter 10.2: Estate Planning and Asset Protection

As you navigate the realm of financial success and wealth accumulation, it is crucial to consider the long-term preservation and protection of your assets. Chapter 10.2 explores the critical importance of estate planning and asset protection in securing your wealth for future generations and mitigating potential risks.

1. Understanding Estate Planning:

- The Purpose of Estate Planning: Discover the objectives and benefits of estate planning, including asset distribution, minimizing taxes, and ensuring your wishes are carried out.
- Key Elements of an Estate Plan: Learn about essential components such as wills, trusts, power of attorney, and healthcare directives, and understand how they work together to protect your assets and provide for your loved ones.
- Choosing Executors and Trustees: Gain insights into selecting the right individuals or professionals to manage and administer your estate, ensuring a smooth transition of assets.

2. Asset Protection Strategies:
- Shielding Assets from Liability: Explore legal tools and strategies to safeguard your assets from potential lawsuits, creditors, and other threats.
- Business Entity Structures: Understand the benefits and limitations of various business entity types, such as corporations, limited liability companies (LLCs), and partnerships, in protecting personal and business assets.
- Insurance as a Protective Measure: Learn about the different types of insurance, including liability, property, and umbrella insurance, and how they can provide an additional layer of protection for your assets.

3. Trusts and their Role in Asset Protection:
- Living Trusts: Discover how living trusts can help manage and protect your assets during your

lifetime and ensure a smooth transfer of wealth to your beneficiaries.

- Irrevocable Trusts: Explore the benefits of irrevocable trusts in asset protection, including shielding assets from estate taxes and potential legal challenges.

- Specialized Trusts: Learn about trusts tailored for specific purposes, such as charitable trusts, special needs trusts, and spendthrift trusts, and how they can protect assets and serve your unique goals.

4. Minimizing Estate Taxes:

- Estate Tax Overview: Understand the basics of estate taxes, including current thresholds and exemptions, and explore strategies to minimize their impact on your estate.

- Gifting and Tax-Advantaged Strategies: Discover the benefits of gifting assets during your lifetime, utilizing annual gift tax exclusions, and leveraging tax-advantaged vehicles like qualified personal residence trusts (QPRTs) and family limited partnerships (FLPs).

5. Regular Review and Updates:

- Importance of Regular Review: Recognize the significance of regularly reviewing and updating your estate plan to reflect changes in personal circumstances, tax laws, and financial goals.

- Seeking Professional Guidance: Understand the value of consulting with estate planning attorneys, tax advisors, and financial planners to ensure your plan remains comprehensive, effective, and aligned with your objectives.

By delving into estate planning and asset protection, you will gain the knowledge and tools necessary to safeguard your wealth, provide for your loved ones, and leave a lasting legacy. Remember, estate planning is a dynamic process that should be revisited and adjusted as your circumstances evolve. With careful preparation and guidance, you can achieve peace of mind knowing that your assets are protected, and your wishes will be honored.

10.3 Giving Back: Philanthropy and Social Impact

In our exploration of profit power, we have focused on the art of making money and building wealth. However, true fulfillment and purpose lie not only in personal financial success but also in the positive impact we can make on the world around us. In this final section, we will delve into the importance of giving back through philanthropy and social impact initiatives.

Philanthropy is the act of using your resources, whether financial or otherwise, to promote the welfare and well-being of others. It provides an opportunity to share your success and make a meaningful difference in the lives of individuals and communities. By engaging in philanthropy, you can contribute to causes that align with your values and passions, amplifying the impact of your profit power.

When considering philanthropy, take the time to identify the issues or areas that resonate with you the most. Whether it's supporting education, healthcare, environmental conservation, or social justice, find a cause that ignites your passion and reflects your desire for positive change. Research organizations and initiatives that are dedicated to addressing these issues effectively and efficiently, ensuring that your contributions have the greatest possible impact.

While financial donations are an important aspect of philanthropy, it's equally valuable to consider how you can leverage your skills, expertise, and networks to drive meaningful change. Your professional knowledge and experience can be invaluable resources for nonprofits and social enterprises working towards social impact. By offering your time, mentorship, or pro bono services, you can amplify your philanthropic efforts and create a lasting legacy.

Moreover, consider the concept of "impact investing," which involves deploying capital in a way that generates both financial returns and measurable social or environmental benefits. Impact investing allows you to align your profit-seeking activities with your desire for positive change, providing a win-win situation where you can make a financial return while also driving meaningful societal progress.

In addition to individual philanthropy, consider opportunities for collaboration and collective action. Joining forces with like-minded individuals, businesses, or organizations can multiply the impact of your giving. Through partnerships, joint initiatives, or collective giving platforms, you can pool resources and expertise to tackle complex challenges and achieve transformative outcomes.

Remember, giving back is not just about the impact you create; it can also bring immense personal fulfillment and a sense of purpose. Witnessing the positive change you contribute to and knowing that you have made a difference in someone's life can be incredibly rewarding. Philanthropy and social impact can become an integral part of your profit power journey, providing a deeper meaning and sense of fulfillment along the way.

As you embark on your philanthropic endeavors, approach them with intention, research, and a long-term vision. Seek guidance from experts in the field of philanthropy or connect with experienced philanthropists who can share their insights and best practices. By learning from those who have paved the way, you can navigate the philanthropic landscape with wisdom and maximize the impact of your contributions.

In conclusion, giving back through philanthropy and social impact initiatives is a powerful way to leverage your profit power for the greater good. By contributing your resources, time, and expertise, you can create a positive legacy that extends far beyond financial success. Embrace the opportunity to make a difference, and let your profit power be a catalyst for positive change in the world.

Conclusion: Embracing the Profit Power Mindset

Congratulations! You have reached the end of "Profit Power: Understanding the Art of Making Money." Throughout this journey, we have explored the intricacies of profit, delved into the mindset required for financial success, and uncovered the strategies and tools needed to harness the profit power within you.

In our modern world, where economic landscapes constantly evolve and opportunities abound, understanding the art of making money is more important than ever. This book has aimed to equip you with the knowledge and insights to navigate these complex terrains and thrive in your pursuit of financial prosperity.

We began by emphasizing the significance of developing a wealth consciousness and overcoming limiting beliefs. By cultivating a mindset rooted in abundance and possibility, you lay the foundation for your success. Remember, your thoughts and beliefs shape your reality, and adopting a positive and proactive mindset is essential in your journey towards financial freedom.

We explored the fundamentals of profit, distinguishing it from mere revenue. Understanding the economics of profit and identifying profitable opportunities are vital skills that empower you to make informed decisions and drive your financial endeavors forward. Moreover, we discussed the power of financial literacy, highlighting its role in enabling you to navigate the complexities of personal and business finance with confidence and competence.

Building a profitable business is a key aspect of our exploration. We delved into selecting the right business model, conducting market research, and developing a compelling value proposition that resonates with your target audience. We also examined effective marketing and sales strategies to attract and retain customers, as well as the importance of prudent financial management to ensure sustainable profitability.

Recognizing the significance of investments, we explored the world of investing and the development of an investment strategy tailored to your goals and risk tolerance. Additionally, we discussed the role of technology in leveraging your profitability, emphasizing the need to embrace digital transformation and harness the power of data and analytics.

We acknowledged the cyclical nature of economies and the importance of identifying and capitalizing on market trends. By mastering strategies to navigate economic cycles and adapt to changing landscapes, you position yourself for success even in challenging times. Furthermore, we discussed the importance of building long-term wealth and leaving a lasting legacy, including estate planning and making a positive social impact through philanthropy.

As you conclude your journey through this book, I encourage you to embrace the profit power mindset. You now possess the knowledge, tools, and strategies to unlock your full potential in the realm of making money. Remember that achieving financial success requires continuous learning, adaptability, and perseverance. Apply the principles and insights shared in these pages, but also be open to new opportunities and remain agile in your approach.

I wish you every success as you embark on your own profit power journey. May you create abundance, achieve your financial goals, and make a positive impact in the world. Remember, the art of making money is not solely about personal gain; it is also about creating a life of purpose, fulfillment, and the ability to make a difference. Go forth and embrace the profit power within you!

www.ingramcontent.com/pod-product-compliance
Lightning Source LLC
Chambersburg PA
CBHW052324220526
45472CB00001B/262